The We
Wealthiest
Losers

The World's Wealthiest Losers

By
Margaret Nicholas

OCTOPUS BOOKS

First published in 1989 by
Octopus Books Ltd
A division of the Octopus Publishing Group
Michelin House
81 Fulham Road
London SW3 6RB

Copyright © 1989 Octopus Books Ltd

ISBN 0 7064 393 76

Printed in Great Britain at The Bath Press, Avon

Frontispiece photographs: Nina Dyer, Elvis Presley, Aristotle Onassis.

Contents

Acknowledgements

With a book such as this, covering a wide variety of characters, the author must draw much of her information from previous works. It would be impossible to mention all of them but the author wishes in particular to acknowledge the following writers:

Raymond Strait and Terry Robinson: *Lanza, his Tragic Life* (Prentice-Hall); Caroline Latham: *Prescilla and Elvis* (Star); Jim Black: *Elvis on the Road to Stardom* (W.H.Allen); Robert Gibson with Sid Shaw: *Elvis, a King Forever* (Blandford Press); Alan Jenkins: *The Rich Rich* (Weidenfeld and Nicolson); Lucius Beebe: *The Big Spenders* (Hutchinson); William Davis: *The Rich* (Sidgwick and Jackson); Barbara Goldsmith: *Little Gloria Happy at Last* (Macmillan); Gloria Vanderbilt: *Once Upon a Time* (Chatto and Windus) and *Black Knight, White Night* (Sidgwick and Jackson); Jon Bradshaw: *Dreams That Money Can Buy* (Jonathan Cape); Philip Van Rensselaer: *Million Dollar Baby* (Hodder and Stoughton); Fred Lawrence Guiles: *Norma Jeane* (Granada); Gloria Steinem: *Marilyn* (Penguin); Janice Anderson: *Marilyn Monroe* (W.H.Smith); Peter Collier and David Horowitz: *The Rockefellers, An American Dynasty* (Jonathan Cape); Gordon Young: *The Fall and Rise of Alfried Krupp* (Cassell); William Manchester: *The Arms of Krupp* (Michael Joseph); Russell Miller: *The House of Getty* (Michael Joseph); Robert Lenzner: *Getty, The Richest Man in the World* (Hutchinson); Nicholas Fraser, Philip Jacobsen, Mark Ottaway and Lewis Chester: *Aristotle Onassis* (Weidenfeld and Nicolson); Peter Evans: *Ari* (Jonathan Cape); Richard S. Lambert: *The Railway King* (George Allen and Unwin); Robert Bernard Martin: *Enter Rumour* (Faber and Faber); Stephen Smith and Peter Razzell: *The Pools Winners* (Caliban Books).

The publishers wish to thank the following organizations for their kind permission to reproduce the following photographs in this book:

Camera Press 2b, 21, 28, 85, 111, 139; The Hulton Picture Company 98; Pictorial Press 118, 120, 128; Rex Features 2t, 32, 58, 67, 75, 80, 85 inset, 93, 106, 111 inset, 153; Frank Spooner Pictures 48; UPI/Bettman Newsphotos 11, 54, 146.

Preface

There is a widely held belief that the very rich are different from the rest of us. How, one asks, can they belong to the same species when they count their money in millions and bob along through life on a sea of champagne? While most people worry about mortgages and how to pay the electricity bill, they don't have a care in the world. Or do they? Look at the lives of the stupendously rich and you will see that they often have to pay a high price for the privilege. Money *can* equal happiness but, as you will find from the stories of people in this book, it often seems to attract chaos and disaster. There are those who can't handle it, those who lose it and those who think it can buy everything. Great wealth is enjoyed most by those who had to create something to get it. Problems start when the riches filter down to heirs who find their lives unmotivated. Some even want to give their money away.

Yes, with their diamonds and furs, their yachts and mansions, their private jets and limousines, the rich *are* different, as American writer F. Scott Fitzgerald once said. But perhaps after reading this book you'll ask 'Who want's to be a Millionaire?'

Chapter One

BORN INTO A FORTUNE

Tragic heiresses . . . born into great wealth, but poorly endowed with the priceless riches of love, emotional stability and real friendship.

'All heiresses are beautiful.'

John Dryden (1691)

Gloria Vanderbilt

As a neglected innocent in a world which put wealth, privilege and pleasure before anything else, Gloria Vanderbilt became one of the most haunting figures of the 1930s. She was only ten years old, and heiress to a fortune, when she made front page news in a scandal-ridden tug-of-war between her beautiful but feckless young mother, Gloria Morgan Vanderbilt, and her powerful millionaire aunt, Gertrude Vanderbilt Whitney. To everyone she became known as the 'poor little rich girl'.

The scandal broke at the time of the great depression in America, when poverty, misery, hunger and broken dreams were the order of the day. But the plight of little Gloria struck a chord that transcended class barriers. Despite the fact that one day she would inherit the Vanderbilt millions, no one envied her. The public eagerly lapped up the more bizarre details of life with the upper crust when the battle for her custody came to court, but they had nothing but sympathy for the round-faced child trying desperately to smile through her ordeal.

Little Gloria, it appeared, had been shunted around the world like an unwanted parcel, too often neglected and forgotten in a world of rich adults pursuing their own pleasure. While they spooned up caviar, she was found to be undernourished; while they dripped with sables and mink, her clothes were often shabby and her shoes scuffed. In later, happier life Gloria wrote that one of her earliest memories was of her mother 'wearing a crystal spangled white gown, looking more fragile and pale than any moonflower and disappearing down an endless hotel corridor.' She remembered longing to take her hand, but did not dare for fear of disturbing the perfect symmetry of long white fingers and scarlet nails. More than anything, she wanted this beautiful creature to take her in her arms and hug her.

Ever since she had been born, on 20 February 1924, little Gloria had had to content herself with being on the fringe of her mother's life. Before her marriage to Reggie Vanderbilt, Gloria Morgan and her twin, Thelma, had been known as 'The Magnificent Morgans'. With their dark hair, magnolia skin and delicate sensuality, they were the rage of American society when they emerged as social butterflies in the season of 1922. They came from a good family, but had no fortune, and their object was to find one. Thelma

Gloria Vanderbilt at 55, a successful designer and author.

crossed the Atlantic to become Lady Furness and mistress to the Prince of Wales. Gloria met and married Reggie Vanderbilt.

At forty-three, Reggie was a hopeless alcoholic who had managed to get through 25 million dollars of his fortune in 14 years. He was short, stout, addicted to gambling and pornography, but still regarded as a brilliant catch by the Morgans. The incredible Vanderbilt palace on Fifth Avenue, where Reggie's mother, Alice, reigned supreme, was enough to convince any girl that she was marrying well. Its 137 rooms included a vast white-and-gold ballroom and a dining-room where 200 guests sat down to 10-course banquets served on the Vanderbilt solid gold service.

During their courtship Reggie behaved like any other rich suitor, buying Gloria mountains of orchids and diamonds from Tiffany's. She did not take in the hard fact that he had spent every cent of his personal fortune and was living on the income of a 5-million-dollar trust established by his father. He could give her the great Vanderbilt name, but her only chance of financial security would be to have a child who would eventually inherit from the trust fund.

After their wedding, Reggie still spent money with abandon, denying himself and his bride nothing. They were constantly on the move, forever entertaining and seldom in bed before dawn. When Gloria gave birth to a seven-and-three-quarter-pound baby girl by Caesarian section, Reggie was so delighted with the new experience of being a father that he slipped a diamond-and-emerald bracelet over his daughter's tiny wrist.

However, once mother and baby had recovered, the new arrival made no difference to her parents' lifestyle. Though reported to be enormously fond of her, they followed the usual pattern of their kind and left her to be cared for by others. From the moment she was born, little Gloria was in the hands of two dominant, unbalanced women. One was her maternal grandmother, Laura Morgan, always referred to as Mamma Morgan, a crazed, hysterical woman who put terrifying ideas into her granddaughter's head; the other was hired nurse Emma Keislich, who became devoted to her charge but obsessively protective. Little Gloria called the latter 'Dodo', looked to her for mother-love and nearly died of grief when she was sacked.

Gloria Morgan had been married to Reggie for two years when his drinking finally caught up with him and he died a horrible death through multiple haemorrhages. She was left in the unbelievable position of being a Mrs Vanderbilt without money. Reggie had not only got through his fortune, but had left enormous debts. It was her baby daughter who would one day become an heiress under a trust fund set up by her ancestor Cornelius Vanderbilt II. And nobody could touch that money until she was twenty-one years old.

Fortunately, Gloria had a meeting with Surrogate Foley of the New York County Surrogates Court. He realized the position she was in, had the power to act and made her a handsome stop gap allowance for the 'support and education of her daughter'. In fact, for a time it was the only money she had to live on. But the rich are never as broke as they think they are, and gradually she received enough from various Vanderbilt sources to leave New York, where she was expected to don widow's weeds, and head, instead, for Paris.

As Mrs Vanderbilt, Gloria had grown used to living in luxury and she didn't intend to change her ways. She shipped her entire household to Paris, where she proceeded to buy a new wardrobe from the top couturiers. Little Gloria was carted around Europe in the wake of her restless, remote, untouchable mother. Years later, she would remember: 'I lived from hotel to hotel until I was eight-and-a-half years old . . .' During one year alone, her schedule was breathtaking. In January she was taken to the Sherry-Netherland Hotel in New York where the Vanderbilts had a luxurious suite, and was left there with her nurse while her mother went to California. In March she was sent back to Paris while her mother went to England. A month later, she was sent for and taken to England, to stay first at a hotel in Maidenhead, then at her aunt Lady Furness's country house, Burrough Court at Melton Mowbray. In May she was hustled off to nearby Gaddesby Hall, where all the people were strangers and she saw no one but Dodo. In June she returned to Paris, where she was put to bed with scarlet fever. Shaky, but recovered, in July she was packed off to the Hotel Victoria in Glion. In August she actually spent two weeks with her mother in Monte Carlo, 'But I saw very little of her,' she wrote in her later autobiography 'She was beautiful and exquisite . . . she was mysterious, remote and unattainable to me . . . the ropes of pearls against the soft velvet of her yellow dress . . . how could I ever reach out and be part of her?'

In the autumn of 1926, the beautiful widow booked a passage for herself and her brother Harry on the *Leviathan*, sailing for New York with Queen Marie of Rumania and her nephew Gottfield, Prince Hohenloe. A romance developed, for Gloria always had a weakness for famous names, and when she returned to Paris she hinted to her mother that she might become Princess of Hohenloe-Langenburg. Mamma Morgan became hysterical. She knew the Prince had no money and became convinced that he wanted to marry Gloria for one reason only – to get her hands on her granddaughter's inheritance.

All her children, including Gloria, thought that Laura Morgan was crazy. She looked weird, with her face powdered white, her hair dyed ginger blonde and half-moon pencil lines replacing her shaven eyebrows. Little

Gloria loved her because she gave her affection, but the old lady became quite obsessed about the child's safety and, eventually, was convinced that her daughter intended to kill her. Once Prince Hohenloe came on the scene she transferred her mad venom and her fears towards him. She came to believe that, once married to her daughter, the Prince would murder little Gloria for her money. Her daughter, she said, would weep 'like a Magdalen', but the child's millions would be hers. These accusations were made with alarming frequency. No one could keep Mamma Morgan quiet. Something of their content must have been passed on to three-year-old Gloria. She became nervous, hyperactive and increasingly hypochondriac.

On the one hand was Mamma Morgan with her crazy fears, on the other Dodo with her smothering, protective nature, continually calling doctors and describing her charge as 'delicate'. Between them, as the years went by, they set up a genuine fear in little Gloria's mind that, somehow or other, she was going to die before she was much older.

When she was eight, the first signs of bitterness crept into the sweet, childish letters she wrote to 'Dear Momey'. Suddenly, she seemed to realize that all the times she was alone, her mother was in gay company, laughing with somebody else. Sometimes she would disappear for cruises or visits for weeks on end. Mamma Morgan had been sent home to New York, but she still wrote to her granddaughter and Gloria answered with touching letters addressed to 'Dear Naney'. In one she wrote: 'My mother said not to write to you but I will not pay any attention to her. She is a rare bease (sic). Well, I will be in dear old New York soon . . .'

It had been agreed that little Gloria should be educated in America, and a school had already been chosen for her. The Vanderbilt trustees began putting pressure on Gloria to bring her home. She was furious at the inconvenience. The child had already spoiled her life by wrecking her chances with Prince Hohenloe, who had gone off to marry Princess Margarita of Greece and Denmark. Now she was being asked to give up her wonderful life in Europe for her daughter's sake.

But in March 1932 they did return, to an America suffering from the effects of the 1929 Wall Street Crash. Bread lines were forming in the streets of New York, thousands of desperate people had committed suicide, and crime was getting out of hand. Since 1929, more than 2000 people had been kidnapped for ransom. Just seven days after the Vanderbilts arrived in New York, the 21-month-old baby son of aviation pioneer, Colonel Charles Lindbergh, was kidnapped and later found in a shallow grave. Everyone was talking about the case.

One morning, an anonymous letter arrived at the Sherry-Hilton Hotel where the Vanderbilts were staying. It contained a threat to kidnap little

Gloria. Mamma Morgan feared the worst and told her daughter she must hire detectives immediately. There had been so much publicity about their return and the Vanderbilt name was associated with such vast wealth that kidnapping was a very real possibility. Gloria called an agency and guards were posted. But she, herself, had no intention of spending the summer in New York. With the excuse that she had to close up her Paris house, she left her child in the care of Mamma Morgan, Dodo and the detectives and returned to Europe.

The old lady was appalled by her granddaughter's condition. She was thin, pale and drawn; she stammered and had a nervous twitch on one side of her face. There were shadows under her eyes. Doctors concluded that her tonsils needed removing; but, before any operation, she had to be brought back to full health.

One evening in May, news came through that the Lindbergh baby had been found buried in woods near Princeton, killed by a blow to the head. Little Gloria heard everything. Later that night she was found writhing on her bed with terrible stomach pains. The doctor, called in to see her, remembered her anguish long afterwards as she pleaded, 'Don't let me die.' He concluded she was in a state of mortal terror, not helped by the two women left to care for her whose constant fears for her safety, expressed aloud, increased her vulnerability.

This was the state little Gloria was in when she was taken to dinner with her aunt, Gertrude Vanderbilt Whitney, a formidable and impressive lady.

Gertrude was the châtelaine of great estates, a wealthy society matron, sculptor and founder of the Whitney Museum of Modern Art. She seemed, to the world at large, cold and patrician but, nevertheless, a woman who would do her duty. In a detailed account of the Vanderbilt-Whitney affair, *Little Gloria – Happy at Last*, Barbara Goldsmith reveals that Gertrude had another self, known only to a few. This other self was 'a bohemian, a hedonist, a sophisticate who accepted bizarre behaviour . . . she was a woman who took lover after lover and gloried in the pleasure they gave her; a woman of immense vanity who created herself as a seductive, exotic, unique personality.'

This complex woman, herself the mother of three children, was disturbed, as others had been, to see how pale, thin and nervous her niece had become. She had not seen a great deal of little Gloria since her brother Reggie had died, and she knew nothing of the child's secret fears, but the maternal instinct in her came to the fore. She arranged for her own doctor to perform the tonsillectomy and promised Mamma Morgan that she would approach Gloria to ask if the child could stay with her out in the country until she regained her health.

BORN INTO A FORTUNE

Gloria had returned from Europe just in time for her daughter's operation, and was delighted by the offer. She intended to return to Paris as soon as possible and the arrangement suited her perfectly.

The day after Gloria sailed, her daughter was driven to the magnificent Whitney estate, Wheatley Hills in Old Westbury, with Dodo and a bodyguard for company. There, Gertrude was waiting for her in the Venetian-style mansion with an indoor gymnasium, swimming pool and tennis court, fine stables and acres of parkland. She was shown the stables, where she could have her own pony, and the bedroom Gertrude had furnished specially for her, next to her own.

After six weeks in the country, little Gloria had gained weight, her colour was better and she caught cold less easily, and Gertrude asked Gloria to let the child stay with her till Christmas. Then the visit was protracted even further, and soon the trustees, doctors, lawyers and even Mamma Morgan were urging her to leave little Gloria in Gertrude's care. Slowly it dawned on Gloria that she might never get her daughter back.

Gloria took a house on 72nd Street and hoped that would convince people she intended to provide a home. But at the same time, the newspapers were full of pictures of her out on the town with millionaire promoter 'Blumie' Blumenthal, flamboyant son of a kosher butcher. He was married, and of dubious character. Vanderbilt guardian and trustee Tom Gilchrist warned that the publicity was not good for her. Gloria wept. She could not get her allowance of $4000 a month unless little Gloria lived with her. How on earth was she going to manage?

Gloria made an attempt to win back her daughter in June 1934, offering to take her to New York, but little Gloria turned white and began to shake. She did not want to live with her mother; she wanted to stay with Aunt Ger. Eventually, the 'don't want' turned to fear – fear that her own mother might kidnap her. Gloria was certain that the child's mind had been poisoned against her. There was only one way she could get her back. She would have to go to court.

The preliminary hearing of the Vanderbilt–Whitney custody case was scheduled for Friday September 28, 1934. Ten-year-old Gloria arrived at the Supreme Court Chambers with clenched hands, grinning nervously. She could only barely understand the fight that had arisen between her mother and Aunt Ger. The two protagonists appeared in black and their best furs, diamonds glittering. For the next six weeks the papers, full of nothing but the Vanderbilt–Whitney trial, laid bare, in mouth-watering detail, the lives of two women who represented the upper, upper crust in America and who bore two of its most famous names.

Day after day, Gloria took the stand to justify her way of life and protest her love for her child. She was the public's favourite. Each day she appeared in court on the arm of her nurse and was portrayed by the Press as a beautiful, pathetic, loving, if somewhat wayward mother. Gertrude, on the other hand, emerged as the tough, powerful older woman who thought that her money could buy anything – 'a haughty matriarch of iron whim'. And between them was little Gloria, forced to face questioning that no child should have endured. She was made to testify for almost two-and-a-half hours and, afterwards, curled up like a foetus in the arms of her bodyguard.

Little Gloria made it quite plain to the court that she wanted to stay with Aunt Ger, that she loved Aunt Ger and did not like living with her mother. In the end it was judged that the life led by little Gloria from the death of her father until June 1932 was 'in every way unsuitable, unfit, improper, calculated to destroy her health and neglectful of her moral, spiritual and mental education . . .'

Custody was given to Gertrude Vanderbilt Whitney. Gloria was led from court in a state of collapse and little Gloria emerged from the trial a celebrity.

Gloria's new life on the Whitney estate included a black pony of her own, six servants to look after her every need, bodyguards, private detectives, but not her beloved Dodo. The nurse's influence was considered claustrophobic, making the child fearful and neurotic.

But now the trial was over, was her happiness assured? It seems not. She could not be consoled for the loss of Dodo and blamed her mother for her removal, though she was not responsible. The aunt she loved so much, having won the case was seldom there. She began spending the week in the city and returned to Wheatley Hills only at the weekend when little Gloria was visiting her mother. She was not a woman who could express affection. Gloria's cousin and closest friend, Gerta, recalled: 'No one cared about her, no one. After that trial everyone simply forgot about Gloria – they let her grow up like a barbarian!'

When she was sixteen, she made a decision that proved how emotionally complicated this whole affair had been. She moved to California to live with her mother. Now a most attractive young woman, it was not long before she was seen around town with famous Hollywood escorts, including Franchot Tone, Errol Flynn and Van Heflin. Obviously attracted to older men, she had an intense love affair with Howard Hughes. While still only seventeen she fell in love with a handsome Hollywood playboy, Pat di Cicco, son of a Long Island farmer, and they were married on 28 December, 1941. But she soon regretted having been so impulsive. Pat di Cicco, in spite of his good looks, expensive clothes and charm, turned out to be a bully and an appalling husband.

Gertrude Whitney, who had violently disapproved of the match, died four months after the wedding. In her will she left her niece a diamond-and-pearl bracelet, known to have been her favourite, and therefore seen as a token of her love.

At twenty-one, Gloria came into her Vanderbilt millions, obtained a divorce from di Cicco and, in a blaze of publicity, married famous conductor Leopold Stokowsky, who was forty-two years older than herself. That marriage, too, would end.

There would be other marriages, and there would also be fulfilment of a different kind. Gloria Vanderbilt began to use her talent as a designer and businesswoman and has since made a huge success in both fields. She also began to write, and produced two magical volumes of autobiography. The relationship with her mother was to remain a stormy one, and there were periods of estrangement. But on her sixtieth birthday, she gave her mother a diamond bracelet. All had been forgiven. Little Gloria was 'happy at last'.

Barbara Hutton

When she was a child, Woolworth heiress Barbara Hutton's favourite game was make-believe. She wanted to be a princess and she wanted to be loved for herself alone. She never outgrew this longing and eventually married seven times, searching for the man who would fulfil her dreams, her valiant prince in shining armour.

Three of her husbands *were* princes and another made her a Countess, but each marital encounter ended in disaster. Eventually her life fell into a pattern. She would fall desperately in love, often with someone who was otherwise engaged; having captured and married him, disappointment would set in, her interest begin to fade. He would be replaced. Her search for this elusive consort lasted a lifetime, so that even when she was sixty, she was capable of losing her heart to a fortune hunter if he treated her like a princess.

In the end, despite her massive wealth, she was just a vulnerable, sick woman riddled with loneliness. 'I inherited everything but love,' she told her friend and biographer, Philip Van Rensselaer. 'I've always been searching for it, because I didn't know what it was.'

Barbara Hutton was born in New York City on 14 November 1912, to the sort of wealth that most of us find hard to imagine. The money was made, prosaically enough, by her grandfather, Frank Winfield Woolworth, who had launched the 'dime stores' in America that later spread throughout the world. By the time Barbara was born, he was already a multi-millionaire. Her first memory was of the 60-roomed white marble mansion of Glen Clove on the North Shore of Long Island, where she used to visit the old gentleman she called 'Woolly'. He adored her. She was a chubby, golden haired child with wide blue eyes and porcelain skin. To please her, he would join in her make-believe and call her 'Princess', ordering the chauffeur to treat her like royalty.

Her parents were an ill-matched pair who did not seem to have much idea of what to do with her. Her mother, Edna, F. W. Woolworth's youngest daughter, was a homely, shy woman who never got used to being rich. When Barbara was only five, she was found dead in her luxurious suite at the Plaza Hotel, New York, and there was talk of suicide. Frank Hutton, her father, was on the other hand a brash, energetic man, a Wall Street broker who drank heavily, gambled and womanized. He showered his daughter with gifts, but plainly found her boring.

Barbara was eventually sent off to a select girls' school to be educated in the social graces. She went on several pre-arranged dates with Yale undergraduates, but was not generally sought after. She blamed it on her plumpness. Most of the fashionable young girls of the time were as slender as blades of grass. Barbara, though pleasing to look at with her fair, shining hair and lovely eyes, was obviously too well-padded. She started the first of the endless dieting regimes that, in the end, destroyed her health. She finally became determined to be thin when she met her first prince . . .

They were introduced to each other by a mutual friend. Prince Alexis Mdivani was already well known on the international social scene. The sixteen-year-old schoolgirl found him devastatingly attractive. He was one of three brothers from Tiflis, in Georgia, who had arrived in Paris just before the First World War with their father, Colonel Zakharias Mdivani. They all became associated with famous beauties. Alexis was an unusual looking man with a wide, Slavic face, deep greyish-green eyes and sandy-coloured hair. A great deal of his attraction lay in his voice, which was heavily accented, throaty and seductive. Like his brothers, he had acquired his title somewhat mysteriously. 'Where they come from anyone with three sheep is considered royalty,' quipped one society wit.

BORN INTO A FORTUNE

The prince's first amorous experience was said to have been with the legendary French cabaret star Mistinguett, and this was followed by a tempestuous affair with the raven-haired American actress Kay Francis. Sixteen-year-old Barbara, desperately trying to lose weight on a diet of black coffee and crackers, was hardly in the same league. He was sympathetic, but unimpressed. She wiped away secret tears and tried not to think about him.

In December 1930, Frank Hutton gave his daughter a coming-out party that would be remembered for decades. Most people were still reeling from the effects of the Wall Street Crash but the Hutton family had emerged almost unscathed, its enormous wealth was so widely and wisely invested. Newspapers recorded the party with acid comment. The celebrations began with a tea for 500 socialites, followed by a dinner for another 500. The main event was on 21 December, when the entire ballroom suite of the Ritz Carlton Hotel was taken over for a ball estimated to have cost 60 000 dollars. Four orchestras played, while a thousand guests drank 2000 bottles of champagne in a setting decorated with 10 000 roses, 20 000 bunches of white violets and a forest of silver birch trees. In the streets outside, people were queuing for handouts of bread and soup.

Having launched his daughter in society, Frank Hutton considered she was now ready to receive offers of marriage from men of distinction and wealth. Prince Mdivani was not quite what he had in mind.

Barbara had met Alexis again at a party given by Paris designer, Jean Patou, in Biarritz. He saw at once that she was no longer the lovelorn schoolgirl, but a sophisticated young woman of considerable style. There was something about them when they were together that alerted the sensitive antennae of party-giver and gossip columnist Elsa Maxwell.

The prince, however, met and married Barbara's friend, heiress Louise Van Alen. That made him even more desirable as far as Barbara was concerned. She stayed in Europe, hung around with the high-flying Mdivani set, and within 18 months had achieved her end: one day, Louise walked in and found her husband in bed with Barbara. By the end of November 1932, their marriage had been terminated in the divorce court, and when Barbara returned to New York, Alexis went with her.

Frank Hutton gave Alexis a very cool reception when he called to pay his respects. Barbara was still under twenty-one, and he made it clear he did not consider a divorced Russian emigrF a suitable bridegroom for his daughter. When he saw the determined glint in her eye, however, he gave in, called an army of lawyers to safeguard her fortune and arranged for Alexis to receive a dowry of one million dollars plus a substantial annual allowance. Considering the prince had just received a million-dollar divorce

Barbara Hutton playing the balalaika at her villa in Tangier.

settlement from Louise Van Alen, he seemed to be doing very nicely from his various romantic attachments.

Barbara insisted on being married in Paris. Huge crowds gathered outside the Russian cathedral of St Alexander Nevsky to see her arrive, icily calm and beautiful in ivory satin with a train 8 feet long. When she emerged as Princess Mdivani, it seemed to her that a childhood dream had come true. It was soon to be shattered.

They left for their honeymoon on the overnight train from Paris in a blaze of publicity and with 70 pieces of luggage between them, everything embossed with a gold crown and Mdivani initials. Their destination was Lake Como, then on to Venice, where they had booked the royal suite at the Excelsior Hotel on the Lido. As the train rushed through the night, the Mdivanis retired to their luxurious sleeping compartment. Barbara slipped into an exquisite chiffon nightdress and turned to Alexis to be admired. Taking a very cool look at her somewhat generous figure, he blurted out, 'Barbara, you're too damn fat!' Then he pulled her to her feet and roughly kissed her lips. 'Come on,' he said coldly, 'let's get down to business.'

Barbara was desperately hurt. Her awareness of her weight problem made his brutal frankness even more painful. Next day, she went on a crash diet that consisted of nothing but three cups of coffee a day and a few crackers. She maintained this punishment of her body for three weeks at a stretch, until she had lost 40 pounds within the first few months of her marriage. Sometimes she looked tired and ill, but as the pounds dropped off her she also achieved a more refined beauty.

On 14 November 1933, Barbara celebrated her twenty-first birthday and came into full and unrestricted control of her immense fortune. It was estimated that if she spent 10 000 dollars a day for the next ten years, she would still only have made a dent in her bank account.

That winter, the Mdivanis decided to take a second honeymoon and slipped off with a few friends for an extended spending spree in Japan, China and India. Barbara was fascinated by the Orient and immersed herself in sight-seeing. Alexis was bored by her enthusiasm – his taste was for night-life, polo, dinner parties and shopping. He dozed off on a bench while she toured the Imperial Palace in Peking, and went into a black mood when she tried to drag him round a Buddhist monastery. He began to have temper tantrums, in which he hurled himself to the floor and screamed when things were not going the way he wanted. Then there was his vanity. Indoors he usually walked around naked, to show off his bronzed, muscular figure; and he bought almost as much jewellery as she did. By the time they returned to her suite at the Ritz in Paris she was writing in her diary, 'I feel bored, bored with Alexis. I feel tired, I feel tired of Alexis.'

It was obvious to those around them that something had gone wrong with the marriage. As rumours spread that the Mdivanis were 'finished', Barbara gave a party to celebrate her twenty-second birthday. The huge Regency ballroom of the Ritz and a series of adjoining rooms were magically converted to look like a street in Casablanca, and 2200 guests danced the night away to the sound of popping champagne corks. Among the guests with a seat of honour at the Mdivani's table was a remarkably good-looking aristocrat named Count Curt Haugwitz-Reventlow, a Prussian-born Dane seldom seen on the international party circuit. When the music started he asked Barbara to dance, and as the orchestra played on they became completely absorbed in each other. Alexis stood on the sidelines fuming, for he recognized the signs of mutual attraction. Barbara had met her second husband.

Frank Hutton decided this time that he would have the foreigner's background thoroughly checked. He was impressed by what he discovered. The Count was a bachelor, whose ancestors had been Danish noblemen for 800 years. He was a fine athlete, brilliant on the ski slopes, but most of his time was spent running the family farm in Denmark. No one could produce a scrap of gossip about him, even though he was considered one of the handsomest men in Europe.

In March 1935, Barbara told Alexis she wanted a divorce and after some tempestuous scenes she set off for Reno, Nevada, to establish six weeks' residence while Count Reventlow went home to Denmark for an audience with King Christian. As a feudal landowner he was expected to seek his monarch's approval before entering into a matrimonial contract.

They were married in a short and simple ceremony which took place at a small, quiet resort overlooking Lake Tahoe. Thirty policemen, special deputies and private detectives were called in to keep the public at a distance. Barbara, looking tense but dewy-eyed, wore a plain yellow print dress with a matching straw hat and carried a nosegay of wild flowers gathered for her by her bridegroom. Reventlow was quiet and withdrawn.

The first nights of their marriage were spent in San Francisco, where Barbara managed to throw an impromptu party for 500 people. After a week, Reventlow complained that they never seemed to be alone and wondered if it was going to be like this from now on. He decided they must leave for their honeymoon in Denmark right away. En route, Barbara learned that Prince Mdivani had been killed in a car crash near Perpignan. Although Barbara remained utterly composed at the news, the Count said afterwards that a shadow seemed to pass across her eyes.

The newlyweds stayed at the Reventlow family's Hardenberg Castle on the stark, misty island of Lolland. Everyone hoped that Barbara would settle down there, but she hated it from the start. The only occasion she remembered with pleasure was a dinner party at which Curt's brother, Heinrich, presented her with an emerald bracelet made specially for her at Tiffany's in New York. She was touched by his thoughtfulness and treasured the gift. But nothing could change her mind. She hated the climate, could not understand the language and became increasingly restless. The honeymoon was cut short and it wasn't long before they were back in Paris at the Ritz Hotel.

Count Reventlow soon became aware of his wife's almost morbid dread of food. Most days were spent fasting. She would smoke incessantly, drink cup after cup of black coffee but only toy with the food on her plate. When she stepped on the scales and found she had gained a few ounces, she would burst into tears. The Count found that her reluctance to eat affected him, and even he no longer enjoyed his meals. He suggested she should visit a dietician, but the problem was deeper than he thought.

By mid-September, Barbara found she was pregnant. Her figure would now increase whether she liked it or not. Once she got over her irritation at not being able to wear the latest Chanel gowns for a while, she confessed to close friends she was hoping for a son.

She decided to have the baby in England, which, at that time, seemed to her a place which represented peace and strength. On 23 February 1936, Countess Reventlow was delivered of a baby boy, Lance, in the bedroom of her rented Regency house in Hyde Park Gardens. The bedroom was equipped like a top London clinic. There were serious complications to the Caesarian birth, and it was a few days before she was able to sit up, smiling wanly on her pillows of white satin and old lace.

After the tragedy of the Lindbergh kidnapping in America in 1932, the thought that the same thing could happen to her baby was always present in her mind. She asked her husband to find them somewhere safer to live.

The Count heard that St Dunstan's Lodge, an elegant estate located in the centre of London, off the outer circle of Regent's Park, had come up for sale. Barbara loved it, but as the house itself had been damaged by fire, she decided to tear it down and build a neo-Georgian mansion in its place. She would call it Winfield House in memory of her grandfather.

Reventlow was staggered by the amount of money Barbara poured into the project. He never got used to her casual attitude towards spending millions. She changed her mind so often during construction that the estimated one million dollars rose to 3 million and finally to 4½ million. Half as much again was spent on furnishings. The third floor was turned into a nursery suite for Lance, with walls lined with pink calfskin. All this was placed behind a 10-foot high spiked steel fence.

Nobody knows quite when the bickering began. The Reventlows had one furious row over the dismissal of a servant, which ended in a physical struggle, after which Barbara booked herself into a nursing home. She tried hard to achieve a domestic lifestyle for the sake of their son, but was defeated by her own restlessness. The Count preferred a strictly regulated life, in which the same thing happened day after day. She became bored, fed up with his lack of humour, his bursts of anger and lack of tenderness. All the romance of their first encounter had gone.

Reventlow still loved his wife, however. He reacted jealously and violently when she became infatuated with Prince Friedrich of Prussia, son of Kaiser Wilhelm II, a tall blond young aristocrat who was in London to learn English by working at Schroeder's Bank. She was slipping away from him, and eventually Reventlow moved into the nearby Bath Club. One day, he received a visit from the family solicitor, who told him that Barbara was anxious to bring the marriage to an end without rancour or ill feeling.

Her next choice of husband, actor Cary Grant, surprised everybody. He was considered a rank outsider in the Hutton stakes. Barbara first met him quite casually aboard the liner *Normandie*. They later encountered each other at social gatherings in London, Paris, New York and Palm Beach. Grant was one of the film industry's highest-paid stars, a matinée idol with stunning good looks. To the first hint of any romance with him Barbara reacted sharply, 'He is just a good friend, nothing more.'

By 1941, the couple could not hide the fact that they were in love. Barbara threw a party, ostensibly for just a few friends, but really to give notice to the females hovering around the star that, from now on, he was out of circulation. They made an incredibly handsome couple; Barbara sleek and blonde, shimmering with emeralds and Cary Grant smooth, tanned, flashing his familiar, shy smile.

They were married quietly on 7 July 1942, in a six-minute ceremony at a summer house retreat on the shores of Lake Arrowhead in the San Bernadino mountains. The omens were good.

At first, Barbara enjoyed being married to Cary Grant. They socialized, gave fabulous parties and seemed very much in love. But soon her old restlessness became apparent. She had won the prize; soon, no doubt, she would be bored. Cary Grant began to resent the constant social buzz; it seemed as though *she* could not live without it. He was up early, worked hard at the studios all day, and when he came home in the evening was not always in the mood to play host or to go out. Sometimes he played up at dinner parties to embarrass her. Friends could see the problem. He was a dedicated professional, and she was just an extremely rich lady with nothing much to do.

There was another problem. Gradually Barbara's wealth and her compulsion to spend began to get on his nerves. Why, he asked her, did they have to have such a huge staff? He could not get used to the staggering bills they had to pay even for such basics as electricity, food and toiletries. Soon, his nagging began to get on Barbara's nerves. She used her insomnia as an excuse to sleep in a separate bedroom.

The marriage ended on 30 August 1945. There was no bitterness and Cary Grant blamed himself for not being more sensitive to her needs. Years afterwards, when they were still friends, he said, 'We know each other better now than when we were married.'

To console herself, Barbara bought a Moorish palace in Tangier – and found herself another prince. Compared with most of the people in her circle Prince Igor Troubetzkoy was poor, but his title, as far as she was concerned, was beyond price. He was the youngest son of Prince Nicholas Troubetzkoy, a favourite of the former Tzar, and his line went back to the 14th century. Soon after their first encounter, Barbara invited him to her suite at the Ritz for dinner. She was in her gayest mood, and he was enchanted. She found herself terribly attracted by his lean, athletic figure, twinkling green eyes and sensitive mouth. Prince Igor, looking back on that night said: 'She phoned – we dined – and my word, how fast!'

Prince Troubetzkoy became a regular visitor at the flower-filled suite at the Ritz and, as a connoisseur of art, was overwhelmed by the treasures he saw there: exquisite Chinese porcelain and jade, paintings by Cezanne, a Botticelli, antique gold snuff boxes and incredible jewels. And as for Barbara – she could hardly wait to become a princess again.

Anxious to avoid the Press, they were married in the tiny Swiss village of Chur, near Switzerland. But on the journey back to Paris, the newspapermen caught up with them and Barbara reported: 'I've never been happier. We will be on our honeymoon for 30 or 40 more years.'

Brave words, but Prince Igor realized how little they meant when they arrived at the Ritz. Once in her suite, Barbara brought him down to earth by stating that they would occupy separate bedrooms: his bedroom was down the hall.

Her new husband was soon made acutely aware of her diet problems, which by now amounted to anorexia. She still drank black coffee, smoked incessantly and would only eat tiny morsels of food. Formal meals were rarely served in her suite and Troubetzkoy had no alternative but to take himself off to restaurants.

Barbara also suffered from terrible insomnia and often spent the night hours telephoning friends in New York, London, Los Angeles and Tangier. All too often, it seemed, she was phoning one Baron Gottfried von Cramm, a German tennis ace. She refused to talk to Prince Igor about her relationship with the Baron; he had actually been in and out of her life for years and was always ready to offer her a shoulder to cry on.

The Troubetzkoys had not been married three months when the Prince began to notice a worrying change in Barbara. She became gaunt and hollow-eyed, her legs were like sticks and her skin was grey. Her doctors blamed her life of semi-starvation and insomnia. She seemed to improve after a summer on the Riviera and in Switzerland, but soon relapsed. Her husband called in one of the world's greatest urologists and he diagnosed serious kidney malfunction brought on by self-neglect.

For a time, Barbara's life was in the balance. She asked her doctor to send a telegram to von Cramm telling him to come at once. Prince Igor began to feel he must have failed her as a husband, yet he loved her very much. Just what did this German tennis player mean to her? Troubetzkoy did not know it, but in a moment of delirium she had confessed her unrequited love for the German. She was already beginning to weary of her fourth husband.

During the two years they were married, Prince Igor spent most of his time pacing up and down hospital corridors, waiting to be summoned. Even when she recovered, he was kept at arm's length. He would sometimes escape from the impersonal luxury of the Ritz and have a sandwich and a glass of beer in a bistro – anything to touch reality. He tried hard to understand her, but in the end had to admit defeat. Thus, there was yet another divorce, and a bitter one, for Troubetzkoy was deeply hurt.

Barbara continued moving restlessly about the world and was seen on more than one occasion with von Cramm. But her friends were staggered when they realized that the new man in her life was international playboy Porfirio Rubirosa. They knew that he had just been dismissed from his post as Dominican ambassador for amorous misconduct and, without salary or expense account, needed financial backing. It was also generally known that he was crazy about the Hungarian actress Zsa Zsa Gabor.

Barbara was impervious to all this. She had decided to marry Rubirosa and even phone calls and telegrams from Cary Grant and Gottfried von Cramm, begging her to think again, had no effect. The marriage took place at the Park Avenue home of the Dominican consul in New York on 30 December 1953. Under her wide picture hat she looked strained and tired, and she admitted, 'I'm so tired, I could die.' In fact, she collapsed and had to go to bed before the wedding party had ended. That night 'Rubi' went out on the town and returned in the early hours with a showgirl on his arm.

Barbara knew from the start this marriage wouldn't work, that she should never have gone into it. She wasn't in love with Rubirosa; she had just wanted to prove she could get any man she wanted.

27

BORN INTO A FORTUNE

Barbara Hutton, Woolworth heiress, in her twenties.

The second night after the wedding, Barbara slipped on the bathroom floor and broke her ankle. While she was confined to a wheelchair, her husband was courting Miss Gabor by telephone as though the marriage had never taken place. After just 73 days it ended, and Barbara fled to the peace of her Moorish palace, with its fountains and sun-filled rooms.

At some time during her brief marriage to Rubirosa, friends had heard her say wistfully, 'I was in love with him for 17 years, then he told me he didn't love me.'

'Who?' a friend asked in surprise.

'My tennis player – von Cramm!'

With the wreck of five marriages behind her, she asked von Cramm to stay with her for the rest of the summer of 1955. The spell of Tangier worked wonders. Barbara seemed to regain her looks and vitality, and when she returned to Paris in the autumn it was to plan their wedding.

On a day of heavy wind and rain, Barbara married her Baron in a civil ceremony at Versailles City Hall. Von Cramm was a nervous bridegroom, but Barbara looked radiant in a blue Balenciaga suit and pearls. 'We should have married 18 years ago. It would have saved me many heartaches,' Barbara told the Press. But even this dream was doomed to be short-lived.

Their first dilemma came when Gottfried tried to get a visa at the American Embassy so that he could spend the winter with Barbara at Palm Beach. The application was rejected. No reason was given, but there had been past indications that the Baron had homosexual tendencies. He was a decent, kind and honourable man but, as far as the American authorities of that time were concerned, unacceptable.

In his biography of Barbara Hutton, C. David Heymann says that Gottfried von Cramm's inability to relate to her at any kind of sexual level created a deep schism. She took it personally, and the dilemma drove them apart. Von Cramm began making long business trips to Germany, and Barbara occupied herself by having dinner parties. Although they did not divorce until 1957, they began to go their separate ways. The collapse of the dream of an idyllic love which she had nurtured for years made her so ill, she lost weight without dieting.

It had all ended so quickly she could hardly believe it. She began to drink heavily and, for a time, mixed with an international crowd that did the same. But, in spite of her disastrous experiences with matrimony, she did not feel happy as a single woman. Before long, she entered into her seventh, and most exotic, marriage.

Barbara met Raymond Doan, a Vietnamese artist who had been educated in France, on a motoring tour of Morocco. He was married. When he invited the whole of Barbara's party to his house for tea, she bought one of his paintings. A few weeks later, arrangements were made for him to have a one-man show in Tangier. When Barbara, fascinated, attended the opening, he showed her an oil painting he had done of her palace, Sidi Hosni. She bought not only this canvas, but the whole of his exhibition.

Her friends were not surprised when Raymond Doan moved into the palace. They had seen how this slim, dark skinned artist had awakened her interest. There was a stillness about him that intrigued her and, besides, she had always been in love with the East.

One day she went to the Laotian Embassy in Rabat. She had heard titles could be bought there and she wanted one for Raymond Doan. They explained she must have been mistaken; they did not go in for selling titles; but an old man on the premises claimed to have one, and she could probably make a deal with him. The deal was struck. Raymond Doan the artist was now Prince Raymond Doan Vinh Na Champassak. The reason was simple. Barbara wanted to marry him, and she wanted to be a princess once more.

The wedding to her seventh husband took place in Mexico in April 1964. After a civil service there was a Buddhist ceremony, for which Barbara dressed in a green caftan trimmed with gold; there were gold rings on each of her big toes and bells round her ankles. Doan wore a white suit with a brilliant swathe of silk over one shoulder. Barbara's friends could see that she was living out a fantasy and wondered how long it would last.

The years that followed were difficult for Doan, a gentle, considerate man. Barbara, increasingly frail and wasted from her lifelong neglect of her health, broke bones easily and suffered from various illnesses. Doan was always there when she wanted him, but she seemed to be drifting further and further away from reality. Eventually, in April 1971, she began to make inquiries about the purchase of an Italian palazzo. She wanted it, she explained, as a going away present for Doan. Those who knew her well realized this meant the marriage was over, and the palazzo a souvenir.

She did not want another divorce. Pathetically, she explained she wanted to keep her purchased title. Raymond Doan's only public statement after the final separation was gallant: 'She gave me much more than money, she gave me love.'

But had she really known what love was? The story of her last years is a story of slow disintegration. She tried for a while to console herself, with an exciting young matador called Angel Teruel, but the liaison did not last long. Her last appearance in public showed an emaciated, frail woman, dripping with jewels, her eyes hidden behind enormous sunglasses. When she died on 11 May 1979, aged sixty-six, there were friends at her bedside – but no husband.

Henrietta Guinness

During the 'swinging sixties', Lady Henrietta Guinness was one of the bright young hopes of the famous Anglo-Irish brewing family and heiress to millions of pounds. It came, therefore, as a great shock to her brother, Lord Iveagh, head of the Guinness clan, when she blurted out: 'I hate the rich man's attitude to life. I'm tired of snobbery. I want to be with real people.'

She threw herself wildly into the classless, rootless life of King's Road, Chelsea, where young London aristocrats in search of a thrill mingled with the 'sixties elite – hairdressers, models, photographers, struggling artists and the so-called 'beautiful people'. It quickly became known that Henrietta cared so little for her money, she was trying to *give* it away. Family lawyers frantically tried to prevent her from dispersing her fortune to all and sundry, but with little effect.

Struggling to free herself from a dynasty that had evolved over nine generations into a formidable social force, its name synonymous with wealth, glamour and privilege, she told her friends: 'If I had been poor, I would have been happy.' But her search for something to replace the rich man's way of life ended tragically when, in 1978, at the age of thirty-five, she committed suicide by throwing herself from an aquaduct in the Italian town of Spoleto.

Henrietta was not the first Guinness to try to break away. The family history is full of eccentrics, missionaries, adventurers, ranchers and sheep farmers. One generation alone produced a pop singer, a champion amateur jockey, a lady who modelled topless for Andy Warhol and two professional authors. Nor has the family escaped its share of tragedy, notably by losing several of its young heirs in a series of fatal car accidents. But there was something especially poignant about the life and death of Henrietta.

For 250 years her forbears had been building up the fortune that is now estimated in hundreds of millions. Their origins were humble enough. It was late in the 17th century when a poor young soldier called Richard Guinness was sent from England to Ireland in the course of duty. He married, left the army and became butler to the Protestant Archbishop of Cashel. One of his duties was to brew beer, a rich dark brew very much like the strong porter favoured by working men in those days. Legend has

31

Reluctant debutante Henrietta Guinness, in London.

it that the water of Dublin's river, the Liffey, gave the beer its special character. Whatever the secret, it was passed down to Richard's son, Arthur, who, in 1756, set up a brewery at Leixip, just across the boundary of County Kildare, with a legacy of £100 left him by the Archbishop. He called the brew 'Guinness', and from him has descended the generations of the great Guinness family. In 1867 a Baronetage was conferred, and in 1919 the head of the family was created Earl of Iveagh.

Henrietta was the daughter of Arthur Onslow Guinness, Viscount Elveden, great-great-great-great-grandson of the founder of the Guinness dynasty and heir to the second Lord Iveagh. Her mother was Lady Elizabeth Hare, daughter of the Earl of Listowel. She never knew her father. Arthur was killed in action in Holland in 1945 at the end of the Second World War. He was only thirty-three and Henrietta was barely two-and-a-half. His widow was left to bring up his son, Ben, who became the present Lord Iveagh, and his two small daughters, Henrietta and Elizabeth.

Henrietta's childhood was that of a super-rich little girl with servants at her beck and call, wanting for nothing. Her mother married again, this time Rory More O'Ferrall of the celebrated family of Irish blood stock breeders and trainers. From then on, the three children were shuttled between great estates in England and the family's much-loved Dublin seat, Farmleigh.

Most of her memories were of the Elveden Estate in East Anglia, which her grandfather had bought from the Maharaja of Lahore and which had been turned into a palatial country house to which kings, dukes and foreign nobility were invited. It had passed the days of its greatest glory and Henrietta was relieved when her mother told her that the family would live in the comfortable Old Rectory in the grounds, only opening the vast 100-roomed mansion for special events. She preferred the beautiful Pyrford Court near Woking in Surrey with its view from the upper storey across 2000 acres of pine trees and gorse. But whether it was at Elveden, at Pyrford, at the family's handsome London house, Gloucester Lodge in Regent's Park, or at Farmleigh, there was always an army of servants to cater for every whim.

Henrietta received the classic education befitting a wealthy heiress, including a spell at finishing school. She emerged from the process at nineteen as a delightful girl who had sparkle, zest for living and a generosity of spirit that was utterly genuine. She was pleasant-looking, but no beauty. Short in stature and inclined to plumpness, she also had the blonde, blue-eyed family colouring and an infectious laugh.

At first, she took part in all the rituals of upper-crust life: balls, champagne parties, weekends at vast country houses, point-to-points. But she showed no interest in the Old Etonians and Harrovians who escorted her, and before long she did not even try to hide her boredom. This was when she told a close friend that she hated the way she was living: 'I'm tired of snobbery and I want to be with real people.'

Leaving behind the life she considered 'meaningless', she sought companionship in the trendy demi-monde of Chelsea, where her friends were other free wheeling young aristocrats, waiters, actors, hairdressers, models and the new wave tinkering with the hippy culture. Her generosity was soon legendary. Never mind how many bottles of champagne they drank; no matter how fantastic the bill, Henrietta would pay. The horrified Guinnesses slowly began to realize that Henrietta was throwing her fortune away. She had a hard core of genuine friends, but there were too many one-night acquaintances and hangers-on.

From the beginning, she seemed fated to have love affairs that brought her nothing but unhappiness. In 1963, she ran off with well-known man-about-Chelsea, twenty-six-year-old Michael Beeby. Nothing came of the affair, but on their return from the south of France they crashed in her red Aston Martin. Both were badly injured, Henrietta nearly losing her life. The effects of that crash, both mental and physical, kept her in and out of nursing homes and clinics for the next two-and-a-half years.

Nothing seemed to go right for her during that period. While in hospital she learned that her closest and best friend, Sara D'Avigdor Goldsmid, had been drowned. The severity of the loss can be judged from the fact that, years later, she named her baby daughter Sara in her memory.

From this time on she was to suffer bouts of depression, but if she found happiness anywhere it was among the trendy Chelsea characters who flocked around her on her return to London life. Overweight and insecure, she grasped at straws for companionship and comfort, always keeping up the façade of 'good old Henrietta'.

Henrietta continued to spend her money wildly and recklessly. Her brother, Lord Iveagh, and the trustees of the Iveagh Estate tried to reason with her. In the end, out of concern for her future and trying to protect her £5 000 000 inheritance, they prevailed upon her to sign it all into an unbreakable lifetime trust. Frederic Mullally, who tells the whole story of the Guinness family in his book *The Silver Salver*, says: 'A portion of it bore regular interest which Henrietta dispersed virtually as soon as – and sometimes before – it reached her bank. It went either in outright gifts, or in hospitality to the mixed company of freeloaders and fair-weather friends who, together with the more genuine variety, made up her court.' At this time, he says, she was smoking 'pot' like the rest of the gang and being ripped off by some of the Chelsea restaurateurs who were happy to pad out her nightly bills in compensation for the behaviour of her retinue.

One restaurant owner who kept a fatherly eye on Henrietta was Alvaro Maccioni. His place at 124 King's Road was considered one of the 'in' restaurants at that time and was always full to the doors. He protected her, as far as he could, and kept her from inviting every Tom, Dick and Harry off the streets for her wildly gregarious suppers.

In 1973, when she was twenty-five, Henrietta fell in love with one of Alvaro's chefs, a tall, handsome young Italian called Benito Chericato. From the moment she set eyes on him she would do anything to be near him. Alvaro could not keep her out of his kitchen. She would wash dishes, polish glasses, chop vegetables, anything to be near Benito. The young chef was flattered, but placed in a most difficult position. Henrietta made no bones about the fact that she wanted to marry him, but Benito already had a girl in his life and they had children.

As a Guinness, Henrietta was used to getting what she wanted. The quiet, unassuming young Italian was bowled over and totally confused. She persuaded him to take her to Italy to meet his parents and even turned Catholic to make herself more acceptable to them. After they were married, she said, she would buy them a hotel–restaurant in northern Italy. They would have the biggest hotel on Lake Garda. 'I don't want him to be a cook all his life,' she told friends. 'He will receive the guests, and I will do the housekeeping.'

Henrietta's plan might just have been the answer to the aching void in her life and would have given her existence real meaning. But Benito was not prepared to marry her and the affair fizzled out around 1969. They remained friends, and she set him up in his own restaurant in Belgravia at the reported cost of £28 000.

Ever since her teens, Henrietta's hairdresser had been Stewart Hiscock, a good natured man in his thirties who proved to be one of her genuine friends. He would often take her home to supper with his wife. They were both very concerned about her and especially about the fact that, in spite of her wealth, she did not have a place of her own. She lived like a gipsy. After a discussion one night she promised to find somewhere, but ended up taking 'a terrible bedsitter' in Rutland Gate, Knightsbridge.

The Iveagh trustees finally agreed to buy her a modest mews house in Belgravia. She took little interest in furnishing it, however, and adorned her windowsills with posies of flowers stuck in milk bottles. But, for a time, she was happy there. She had switched her enthusiasm from the Chelsea scene to London's art galleries and studios, where she enjoyed the company of modern painters and sculptors, bought works by Hockney and Nolan, but had to be restrained from buying up whole collections when she took a fancy to the work of an unknown artist.

BORN INTO A FORTUNE

In 1976 Labour Chancellor of the Exchequer, Denis Healey, announced his policy to 'soak the rich', and the Iveagh trustees pressed Henrietta to go into tax exile to save her fortune. Though she claimed she cared little for her money, they pointed out she really had no alternative. Her almost manic generosity, together with the annual tax burden on her unearned income, had ruled out any chance of her accumulating any savings. The trustees clamped down on the release of further chunks of her capital.

Henrietta's trustees finally suggested she go on a world tour – but her heart was really in Italy. She loved the Italian people and made up her mind to go to Rome. She could live happily on her income there and might persuade the guardians of her wealth to allow her enough capital to buy a small house. Her friends could then fly out to join her for weekends.

Before she left for Italy, Henrietta made another of her stunningly generous gestures. A year after buying the Belgravia restaurant for Benito Chericato, she had gone into partnership with Stewart Hiscock, setting him up on his own in an elegant hair salon just off Kensington High Street. He thrived, numbering among his clients Mrs Michael Heseltine, Rex Harrison's wife, Elizabeth, and the Countess of Normanton. Her last act before leaving England was to hand over her share of the £70 000 business to the astounded Hiscock.

A Lady in her own right since her brother had become the third Lord Iveagh, Henrietta was more than ever a rebel against the Tatler lifestyle enjoyed by most of the Guinness clan. But she had not really found another answer and was prone to bouts of illness and depression. When she set off for Rome, she took with her only the things she prized the most. One of her most valued possessions was her favourite Porsche car. She had a few Hockney and Nolan paintings, which she took with her wrapped in Irish linen sheets. There was a silver kettle, a valuable necklace her grandfather had left to her and some pearls, which she valued highly because her brother Ben, Lord Iveagh, had given them to her for her twenty-first birthday. But she took very little money.

When she first arrived in Italy, Henrietta suffered one of her periods of depression. Friends in Rome, not understanding how delicate was her mental health – a legacy of that awful car crash in the South of France –arranged parties to welcome her into the smart set. It was the last thing she wanted. She took herself off to a quiet, back-street hotel where she could be alone and think about the future.

When she had been in Italy for about a year, she heard about a famous Arts Festival held annually in the lovely old town of Spoleto, about 75 miles north of Rome. She decided to spend a few days there.

Among the thousands who attended the Festival, Henrietta had eyes for only one. He was a tall, good-looking, quietly spoken Italian called Luigi Marinori, an ex-medical student who had a temporary job as a waiter at the Festival. Henrietta spoke fluent Italian. She was attracted by him and made no secret of it. They arranged to see each other again and were soon deeply in love.

Henrietta abandoned Rome so that she could be with Luigi, and before long moved in with his family. This meant living with Luigi's father, who was a metal mechanic, his mother, who worked as a chambermaid, his brother and his grandmother. The Guinness heiress seemed very happy at last. The Marinori house was a shabbily built modern villa with green shutters in a dowdy section of Spoleto overshadowed by towering council blocks. But there were bright red pelargoniums in pots outside the door and the six rooms of the house were sparkling clean and full of life. She behaved like any other Italian girl living at home, helping Luigi's mother with the washing, shopping and making pasta.

For a long time, Luigi said nothing to his parents about Henrietta's background. They were completely unaware that she was an heiress with a title of her own and a fortune accumulating year by year. He didn't seem at all interested in her money. In 1977, when she was thirty-five she gave birth to Luigi's child, a beautiful little girl whom she called Sara. Three months after the birth, they were married, quietly, in a civil ceremony at Spoleto Town Hall.

Henrietta tried hard to remain anonymous in Spoleto. She dressed simply, helped her mother-in-law with the housework and seemed to be a devoted wife and mother. The only thing that distinguished her from the other Italian wives in that part of town was that she drove around in a brand new blue Fiat. But when her mother, Lady Elizabeth, turned up in a chauffeur driven car to see her new granddaughter, tongues began to wag. Luigi, they realized, was a very, very lucky fellow.

After the birth of Sara, Henrietta suffered a fresh bout of depression and she entered a local clinic for treatment. Once she was well again, the future seemed to hold a great deal of promise. Luigi had a job as a truck driver. She had persuaded the trustees to give her £26 000 of her capital to buy a crumbling old monastery on the outskirts of Spoleto and she planned to turn it into a comfortable home for herself, Luigi and Sara. All she wanted was a peaceful, tranquil life.

One beautiful May morning in 1978, Luigi took the wheel of the Fiat and drove Henrietta to see her dentist, Signor Giorgio Mastropiero, promising to pick her up later. When he returned she had already left, and the dentist said she seemed to be in a confused state.

Some dark force inside her led Henrietta to the 14th-century Bridge of

Towers, which looms over an old Roman aquaduct and the Tessino River. A young couple saw her, wearing a dark blouse, white skirt and knee-high boots, but she had plunged to her death before they could reach her. She left her handbag behind. It contained a photograph of her baby, a bank book showing a £400 deposit, an address book full of English names and a letter from a friend.

The tragedy brought the families of Guinness and Marinori together in grief. At the funeral, Lady Elizabeth was seen to be trying to comfort the baby's Italian grandmother. There was a simple funeral service at Spoleto's 1500-year-old San Salvatore Church and the burial took place in the adjoining cemetery. Luigi Marinori was too stricken to speak. He had cared nothing for his wife's fortune, said his family. He had loved her. But not even he had been able to give her peace of mind.

Everyone expected a legal wrangle, with an ugly tug-of-war over little Sara Marinori, but matters were arranged quietly and decently. The Guinness family agreed to Sara being brought up by her father in Spoleto until the time came for her to inherit her mother's fortune. She was only six months old when Henrietta fell to her death. At that time the inheritance was worth in the region of £5 000 000, but it is estimated the money will be worth nearer £25 000 000 by the time Sara is twenty-one.

What will it mean to her? What *can* it mean to her? Brought up in a simple, loving Italian family where a new bicycle is a thing to be looked forward to and treasured, money on this scale will be hard for her to grasp. But one day, she too will be a Guinness heiress. In London, a friend of Henrietta was quoted as saying, 'I only hope her inheritance will bring her more happiness than it brought her mother.'

Evalyn Walsh McClean

Washington hostess Evalyn Walsh McClean had such a passion for diamonds that, in 1911, she begged her millionaire husband to buy her one of the most infamous gemstones in the world. It was the Hope diamond, often more aptly called the Diamond of Despair.

Mrs McClean, a renowned collector who already owned the fabulous 100-carat Star of the East, refused to believe there was anything sinister about the Hope diamond, anything that could bring her bad luck. She was quite undaunted by the trail of tragedy that had followed the diamond for three centuries like some foul miasma; she only saw its beauty.

When the diamond was first shown to her by jeweller Pierre Cartier, Evalyn did not like the setting but confessed she was mesmerized by its strange deep blue light. Her husband, Edward McClean, the newspaper tycoon, agreed to buy it for a price said to be in the region of £60 000. He had it re-set and hung on a thick diamond-studded chain.

Since Evalyn McClean was one of the richest and most famous society hostesses of her day, the purchase of the Hope diamond made front page news. So, too, did the tragic events that followed. Her only son was killed in a motor accident. The marriage to Edward McClean went wrong and they were divorced – he was later admitted to a mental home, where he died penniless. Her daughter died from an overdose of sleeping drugs and two women friends who borrowed the diamond also died sudden and unexpected deaths. Evalyn, herself, ended life in a haze of drink and drugs, with much of her great fortune gone.

Even before the Hope diamond appeared in her life, Evalyn Walsh McClean's story was one of incredible wealth tainted by disaster.

She was the daughter of an Irish immigrant carpenter, Tom Walsh, who had left Clonmel, Tipperary, to escape the famine of the 1850s and struck gold in the mountains of south-western Colorado. On arrival in the New World, Tom had found work on the Colorado Central Railroad. But he soon succumbed to the gold fever that was in the air and joined thousands of others prospecting in the Black Hills with varying luck. He married, turned his hand to hotel keeping in Leadville, then began prospecting again. This time, he went out to a remote, desolate area behind Red Mountain.

where no one had ever prospected before. He found a vast fissure of tellurium gold, where only silver lead carbonates had been found previously. Within a year, Tom Walsh's Camp Bird Mine was one of the greatest gold producers in the Western Hemisphere.

Evalyn was born on 1 August 1886. She was twelve years old when she began to realize that her parents were rich beyond most people's wildest dreams. Tom Walsh was making money at a stupendous rate and had no desire to hide his light under a bushel in Leadville, Colorado, or even Denver for that matter. He rented a vast suite of rooms at the old Cochran Hotel in Washington for the season and fitted out his womenfolk in appropriate style. Mrs Walsh, refined and ladylike, was draped in furs that made other women faint with envy. Little Evalyn asked for, and got, a blue Victoria carriage of her own, drawn by a pair of sleek sorrels and accompanied by a coachman in livery.

Politically astute, Tom Walsh set out to make sure he knew the right people. He and his wife entertained lavishly, in great style, and contributed to all the right charities. President McKinley could not help but be impressed, and in 1899 he sent Tom Walsh to Paris to be a commissioner at the Paris Exposition. Little Evalyn went too, and fell in love with France, its sophistication, luxury and style. She was most impressed by the private train in which she and her parents travelled to visit King Leopold of the Belgians. Each carriage was as big as a room, hung with costly paintings, the floors strewn with rare oriental rugs. Liveried servants were constantly at her elbow offering delicacies of the most expensive kind. She made a vow that she would travel in splendour until the day she died.

On their return to Washington, Tom Walsh decided to build a house that would reflect his fantastic success, and a five-million-dollar mansion was commissioned on the luxurious Massachusetts Avenue. As a teenager, Evalyn drifted about the 60-roomed house, which had a grand staircase guarded by marble nymphs, a theatre, a ballroom and a spectacular reception hall with a well that soared four floors upwards to a dome of coloured glass.

She was sent to a finishing school in Paris with a letter of credit from her father which, besides allowing her $10 000 for basic expenses, also gave her credit at all the best shops, including Cartier the jewellers. After a few months, however, Tom Walsh heard that his daughter was spending a good deal too much time among aspiring young artists on the Left Bank and had promised many of them financial backing. Evalyn was ordered home. Before leaving Paris she went shopping and arrived home with eight trunks full of dresses from Worth and Paquin and some magnificent furs, including a sable coat with matching scarf and muff.

The next time Evalyn visited Europe, this time Italy, her father went along as chaperone. High spirited, wilful and attractive, Evalyn was much sought after by handsome young Italians from families with high-sounding titles but no money. When a flirtation with an Italian prince looked as though it might get out of hand, Tom Walsh made a bargain with his daughter. If she would get rid of the prince, he would buy her a car.

Like all the young rich at that time, Evalyn was mad about cars and happily clinched the deal with her father, choosing a smart, red Mercedes roadster. At the time it seemed such a delightful toy. Little did she realize that the pretty red car was the first fateful link in a lifetime chain of disasters.

In 1905, back home in America, Tom Walsh decided to establish a family residence in Newport, which at that time, according to Lucius Beebe, who has recorded the affairs of the super-rich in *The Big Spenders*, was the 'ultimate citadel of New York society'. He bought a house which had once belonged to William Waldorf Astor and was popularly supposed to 'reek with bad luck'. The Walshes didn't believe in such things and launched their new lives there on a sea of champagne.

One fine summer's day, Evalyn set out from the Astor house to attend a clam bake in her precious red Mercedes. Her chauffeur took the wheel and a crowd of young people, full of fun and high spirits, clambered in the back. On the return journey, her brother Vinson sat beside the chauffeur and she rode in the back with a couple of boyfriends. As they were crossing a wooden railed bridge, the Mercedes blew a tyre, ploughed through the rails and crashed upside-down in the stream below. Evalyn, trapped in her seat, was nearly drowned before passers-by managed to pull her free. But her brother Vinson was dead, his body pierced by an enormous splinter that had been sheared off by the bridge on impact.

Evalyn never fully recovered from the effects of that appalling day. Her leg was badly fractured and never properly set. She was in such agony that morphine was prescribed and she became addicted to it. After a series of highly delicate operations she was left a nervous wreck. Some of her hair fell out and a patch at the back remained quite bald. For the rest of her life she had to wear a succession of wigs and take drugs whenever the pain in her leg became too bad.

The Astor house at Newport held nothing but painful memories. Once Evalyn began to walk around, it was felt that perhaps a move back to Colorado might be a good idea. Tom Walsh bought an estate south of Denver, named it Clonmel, after his birthplace in Ireland, and again gave a huge party to declare his faith in the future. But even he began to have doubts when he was nearly killed in a railway accident on his way to inspect new gold diggings in the Colorado mountains.

41

In July 1908, Evalyn caused a sensation by her marriage to Edward Beale McClean. His family owned the *Washington Post* and were considered aristocrats, a cut above the 'new rich'. They had first met as teenagers, when their parents sent them to dancing class, and had kept up a mild flirtation ever since. Ned McClean had proposed to Evalyn at regular intervals, but she did not take him seriously until that summer of 1908. Both were spoiled children, brought up in unbelievable luxury, but Tom Walsh had made some attempt to make Evalyn aware of the rest of the world. Ned's mother, on the other hand, had ruined him, even paying his friends to let him win at games. She was looking forward to seeing her boy married at a wedding of 'cosmic proportions', says Lucius Beebe. But the two young people had other ideas. Out driving one day, Ned begged Evalyn to marry him without delay, by special licence. A few phone calls to influential people and the ceremony was arranged at St Mark's Episcopal Church in Denver. Evalyn could not even remember the name of the clergyman who tied the knot.

Both families were furious, but once the dust had settled arrangements were made to send them on honeymoon in style. The father of the bride and the father of the bridegroom each produced letters of credit for $100 000. The combined sum today would be worth about one million dollars. The happy couple set sail for Europe, where they spent the whole lot in two months.

Seldom can a couple have celebrated with such abandon. They had shipped Ned's favourite yellow Packard roadster from the States with them, but in Paris acquired an additional Mercedes, and later, considering one Mercedes insufficient, bought another. They had a chauffeur, a valet, and a personal maid for Evalyn as well as a mountain of luggage. Evalyn added to the mountain as she purchased furs and couture dresses by the score. Ned had bought her a travelling case fitted out in solid gold, but it had been forgotten, left behind, only to be discovered years later in a cupboard thick with dust.

Part of their honeymoon was spent in the Middle East, and whilst in Turkey they asked the US Ambassador to introduce them to Sultan Abdul Hamid. A meeting was arranged, with all the necessary courtesies, and Evalyn was taken to the harem to be entertained by the Sultan's favourite, Salma Zubayaba. As they drank dark, pungent Turkish coffee out of gold filigree cups, Evalyn's eyes were fixed on Zubayaba's throat. Against the dusky skin lay a fabulous gem stone, deep blue in colour and of the greatest brilliance and purity. It was the Hope diamond.

'I'd give the world to have it, Ned,' Evalyn said as they left the palace. But several deaths had yet to take place before it came into her hands.

The doting young husband whisked her off to Cartier's in Paris to buy her another diamond instead. She was lucky. Just at that moment, a pear shaped diamond, known to experts all over the world as Star of the East, had come up for sale and, at 600 000 francs, was waiting for a rich collector. The McCleans did not have enough money with them to pay for it, so it was charged to Tom Walsh's account. There is no record of what he said when he got the bill, but Evalyn was convinced he would understand she just had to have it.

After the honeymoon the McCleans settled down in Massachusetts Avenue, Washington, for a short spell of domesticity. Their son, Vinson, was born in 1909 and placed in a gold crib sent by King Leopold of Belgium. Nurses and bodyguards watched over the child day and night in case of kidnap, for there had been several threats. But the lull in their frantic social life was short-lived. When her father died of cancer, Evalyn was freed from parental restraint and took off with Ned on a binge around Europe. They were seen at all the fashionable places, spending money like it was going out of fashion.

One of their escapades shocked even the most blasé of their rich friends. Evalyn had been exceptionally lucky at the Casino in Monte Carlo and wanted to return to Paris immediately to spend her winnings. Ned said he would drive her there in his yellow Fiat. The chauffeur could sit in the back. He took on a bet that he could get there before the Blue Train, at that time one of the fastest trains in Europe. He won the bet, arriving in Paris ten minutes before the scheduled express. Celebrations were muted however; the poor chauffeur had had a heart attack and was found dead in the back of the car. Ned's driving had proved too much for him.

Next morning, as the McCleans were at breakfast in their suite at the Bristol Hotel, Pierre Cartier, the jeweller, asked to see him. In his hand was a small package sealed with red wax. It contained the Hope diamond. It's last owner, the Sultan who had received the McCleans in Constantinople, had shot dead his favourite wife in a fit of rage and had, himself, been deposed. The diamond went to a Greek broker, who was killed with his wife and child when his horse and carriage bolted over a precipice. Now it was in Paris in the hands of Cartier. Though he warned Evalyn of its terrible history she answered with a laugh, 'Bad luck objects are lucky for me. Anyway, I don't believe there is such a thing as a jinx.'

The fantastic blue diamond had first been discovered in 1642 by French explorer Jean Baptiste Tavernier. Some accounts say that he bought it in the rough from a mine on the banks of the Kistna River in India, but the more romantic version of its discovery says he stole it from a Burmese temple where it was embedded in the forehead of the god Rama-Sita.

However he came by it, it did him no good. After selling it to the French Bourbon King, Louis XIV, he died penniless, disgraced and in exile.

The stone was then passed down to Louis XVI who gave it to his queen, Marie Antoinette. Both of them died on the guillotine. Marie Antoinette's friend, the Princess de Lamballe, who had worn it on occasions, was torn to pieces by the mob.

The diamond turned up next around 1800 in the possession of a Dutch diamond cutter named Fals, who shaped it into its present form. Fals's son stole it and the cutter died of grief. In remorse, the son killed himself.

Eventually, the stone was bought by Henry Thomas Hope, an English banker, who gave it its name. Henry Hope escaped any evil consequences but his grandson, Sir Francis Hope, had a disastrous marriage and died destitute. The next owner, a French financier, went mad and eventually committed suicide.

So the terrible toll went on, until more than 20 people associated with the stone had met with disaster. In 1908, the diamond was sold to a Russian nobleman, Prince Kanitovski. He gave it to his mistress, Mademoiselle Ladue, one of the stars of the *Folies Bergère*. She was shot in the theatre by a spurned lover and, two days later, the prince himself was stabbed to death in a Paris street. The jewel eventually came into the hands of Sultan Abdul Hamid and then, through Cartier, to Evalyn Walsh McClean.

To celebrate the acquisition of the Hope diamond, Evalyn gave a dinner party at the house in Massachusetts Avenue, which was talked about for years afterwards. It was said even *she* was startled by the size of the bill. There were 48 for dinner, which was served on gold plate with 4000 yellow lilies from England decorating the table. The champagne glasses had stems 12 inches high.

For the next period of their lives the McCleans lived like royalty. They bought country estates and town houses as casually as an ordinary person would buy a pair of gloves. Their favourite country residence, Black Point Farm at Newport, had a staff of 30 for the house and as many more for the grounds and stables. At home in Massachusetts Avenue, Evalyn had commandeered the whole top floor – a space as big as a park – for her personal wardrobe. Her ballgowns and furs alone took up the space of an ordinary sized room.

But things had started to go wrong.

Evalyn adored her first son Vinson, whom she had named after her brother killed in the wooden bridge accident. Nothing was too good for him and the American Press referred to him as the 'one million dollar baby'. Entire performances of the Ringling Brothers circus were bought out so that he might be the only one in the audience and have all the acts performed just for him. Dressed in ermine, cossetted and pampered, he still could not escape his fate. Soon after the purchase of the Hope diamond, Vinson was killed in a car accident.

Nothing was more therapeutic, as far as Evalyn was concerned, than spending money. After Vinson's death she lived more flamboyantly than ever, though friends knew she had suffered greatly. She never went to bed, if she could help it, before six or seven in the morning and hated to be alone. On a visit to New York, for instance, she would take a suite at the Waldorf, invite 100 people in for cocktails then take them all to a championship boxing match.

Her marriage to Ned McClean had entered stormy waters. He was constantly being hounded by his creditors, and eventually he gave up trying to cope with life any longer and was admitted to a mental institution, where he later died.

As she grew older, Evalyn had to face the fact that she had spent a vast fortune in her lifetime and the well was beginning to run dry. Although the Depression of the 1930s made her feel miserable, she did not really understand the financial problems of ordinary people. When depressed, she knew of only one way to make herself feel better. Once, she took a train to New York, where her old friend Pierre Cartier, who happened to be over from Paris, promised to find something to cheer her up. Like a magician, he produced a dazzling ruby-and-emerald bracelet with a 16-carat diamond, known as the Star of the South, as its centre-piece. 'I felt like a new woman the moment he put it on,' she recalled in her memoirs. 'There's nothing like spending money as a cure for not having it.'

By 1947, Evalyn's health was beginning to show signs of strain and she took pain killers as a matter of course. However, nothing could deaden the agony of what happened that summer, when her daughter Evalyn Beale McClean, who had married Senator Robert R. Reynolds of North Carolina, a man much older than herself, was found dead after taking an overdose of sleeping pills.

Not long afterwards, at the comparatively early age of sixty-one Evalyn herself died of pneumonia. She had always predicted that she would die bankrupt, and almost did, as her estate was probated at a mere $606 000.

The Hope diamond was left jointly to her six grandchildren, but they were never allowed to touch it. Meanwhile, it remained one of the most wanted gems in the world. The Russian government was said to have opened negotiations for it, but the deal fell through and the stone was sold to Harry Winston, famous New York diamond dealer. In 1958 he gave it to the Smithsonian Institute in Washington to form the basis of what he hoped would become a famous collection.

No doubt, the McClean family thought the Hope diamond and its sinister legend was out of their lives for ever. But in December 1967, twenty-five-year-old Evalyn McClean, lovely young granddaughter of Evalyn Walsh McClean, was found dead at her home in a suburb of Dallas, Texas, where she lived alone. There was no sign of violence. Neighbours broke into the house after seeing no activity for several days, and found her dressed in jeans and a sweater on the bed . . .

Chapter Two

HOW NOT TO ENJOY A FORTUNE

Be they misers, or simply crack-
pots – some people just don't
seem to know how to enjoy their
wealth . . .

'A moderate addiction to money
may not always be hurtful; but
when taken in excess it is nearly
always bad for the health.'

Clarence Day (1921)

Howard Hughes

I n a penthouse bedroom in Las Vegas, a solitary man sits in a darkened room. He is eating chicken soup. It has taken him hours to consume a few mouthfuls because he is absorbed in an old Western film being run on his private screen. His naked body is emaciated, and both hair and beard hang in lank strands as far down as his waist. His nails are like talons. Every now and then, one of his aides creeps in to remove the soup bowl and reheat the contents, which have gone cold. According to instructions, he averts his eyes and does not say a word. When the bowl has been removed for the last time, the long-haired man covers every surface with paper tissues in case germs have been brought in. Howard Hughes, billionaire, has dined for the day.

Only a handful of people knew how the once famous man-about-town had chosen to live when he disappeared from the social scene in 1952 after a series of legal wrangles. Those few were sworn to silence. The success of his self-imposed seclusion can be guessed from the fact that most people thought he was dead. But Hughes spent the last 15 years of his life in darkened rooms, moving from one to another at the dead of night. His diet was so appalling that he suffered from acute malnutrition. For months at a time he would live on just one kind of junk food, perhaps something he'd seen advertised on television. Once, he went for weeks eating nothing but candy bars and nuts washed down with glasses of milk.

No one knew what had changed him from a handsome tycoon, who had made a massive fortune from his TWA airline, his Las Vegas hotels and Hollywood films; a man who had escorted some of the most beautiful women of the time. Secrecy shrouded that, as it did everything else. 'He hid his own motives so that even those closest to him did not know why he was doing what he did,' says James Phelam, the American investigative writer who, in the end, came as near to the truth as anyone.

Howard Hughes was a Texan. He was born in Houston on Christmas Eve, 1905. His father had become rich by making drilling tools for the oil industry. When he died he left the company to Howard. The young tycoon, however, had a taste for the bright lights and preferred Hollywood to Houston. The film industry was just taking off when he arrived there and he was able to cash in on it immediately. He became an independent

One of the last photographs taken of Howard Hughes.

producer, and within two years scooped up an Academy award. He produced *Scarface*, one of the classic gangster films of all time and *Hell's Angels*, the picture that introduced Jean Harlow, the original platinum blonde, to the world.

At that time Hughes was tall, dark and handsome. Women found him very attractive, but if they chose to throw in their lot with him he would insist they abide by his rules. Any girlfriend he wined and dined was treated with lavish hospitality. She might, if she was lucky, be bought an apartment where she could receive him. But she was forbidden to ask questions and had to be available according to his whim. In typical fashion, he escorted Jean Harlow once or twice, bought her a fabulous apartment, then forgot her. During the 30s and 40s he sometimes had as many as 20 film-struck starlets waiting around for him. At the same time, he was escorting established beauties like Elizabeth Taylor, Lana Turner, Ava Gardner and Joan Fontaine.

His genius for business extended far beyond the range of films. He had a passion for flying and formed two aircraft companies, Trans World Airlines and Hughes Aircraft. During the Second World War he decided to make his contribution to the war effort by building planes. One of them was a giant, eight-engined flying boat which was designed to carry 700 passengers. It only took off once. The second, an experimental long-range reconnaissance plane for the American Army, crashed with Hughes at the controls. The injuries he sustained left him in pain for the rest of his life and made him dependent on drugs.

Hughes married twice. His first wife was Ella Rice; his second, the lovely young actress Jean Peters. She married him in 1957 and told later how she became almost like a prisoner in the luxurious Bel Air mansion he bought for her. The first signs of strangeness were becoming apparent. He insisted they used separate bedrooms and separate *refrigerators*. No one, not even his wife, was allowed to touch his food. He ordered the same dinner every day and helped himself: steak, salad and peas. He had a thing about the peas –they *had* to be small or he would push them away with his fork. The marriage came to an end with a one-million-dollar settlement.

From this time on, he began to fear all kinds of things. Germs were the worst horror. He once told a newspaperman: 'Everybody carries germs around with them. I want to live longer than my parents, so I avoid germs.' His secret weapon was the paper tissue. He kept a huge stock of them by his side. He also had an intense fear of robbers; that was why he never carried any money. He would pay taxi drivers with IOUs and borrow coins from friends when he wanted to make a phone call.

With the end of his marriage, Hughes seemed to become more and more averse to human contact. Sometimes, in order to get away from everything, he would go 'walkabout', taking his provisions in a paper carrier. He bought a bungalow in the desert near Las Vegas and hired a group of five men, all Mormons, for the sole purpose of keeping him from being contaminated by germs.

However strange his behaviour, his business sense was still as sharp as ever and he held secret meetings to discuss million-dollar deals. On one occasion he suspected that his room had been 'bugged', so he made new arrangements: 20 new Chevrolet limousines were ordered; from now on he would meet important business contacts in his car. Why twenty? 'No one will be able to bug 20 cars, and no one will know which one I'm going to use!' was his reply.

By the time he reached his mid 50s, the compulsion to hide from the world became even greater. For the next 15 years he was only prepared to live in the penthouse suites of luxury hotels. The higher the hotel, the better. For himself he would select one small room, which would be given the Hughes treatment: the window darkened with heavy curtains or blinds, the door sealed, a TV set and cinema screen fixed up, papers, magazines and boxes of tissues stacked on top of one another in a corner.

Hughes never stayed in one place for long. After three months at the Desert Inn on the Las Vegas strip, he ordered his entourage to pack up and taken him somewhere else – the Bahamas, Canada, England, Mexico, Nicaragua, it didn't matter as long as no one saw him. Charter pilots on these routes were ordered not to look in Mr Hughes direction when he was taken on board.

The constant travelling with his inner circle of Mormon aides and bodyguards cost a vast amount. He paid high wages to buy loyalty and secrecy. As 'Spot Howard Hughes' had become almost a national game, the entourage, when in transit, had to hustle in and out of undignified back entrances and through hotel kitchens.

In December 1972, Hughes was caught up in an earthquake in Managua, the capital of Nicaragua. The hotel where he was staying shook violently as he lay naked on the bed. His aides came to the conclusion that they had better move quickly before the hotel caved in on them, and hastily bustled 'the boss' into his old bathrobe and a pair of sandals. In all the chaos, he was said to have been calmer than any of them.

From there he sought peace and quiet at London's Inn on the Park. Here, the news came through that thrilled him, news he had been waiting for for 12 years. The US Supreme Court had decided that he was 'Not Guilty' on charges of imposing self-serving deals on TWA. The 170-million-dollar judgment that had been hanging over his head was dismissed.

Suddenly he announced he wanted to fly again, and his whole entourage had to comb London for an old leather flying jacket and a snap-brim Stetson. His hair and beard reached to his waist – it hadn't been cut for three or four years – and a barber was called to make him look trim. Before the barber entered the darkened room he had to 'scrub up' like a surgeon. Anxious aides advised him to wear rubber gloves because of Hughes's phobia about germs. But as the barber began cutting, the gloves were spotted. 'Take the damn things off,' grunted the billionaire. 'Nobody can cut hair with rubber gloves on.' When all the preparations had been made, Hughes finally took off, co-piloting a private jet. He enjoyed it and, for a moment, he was back to reality. But a few weeks later, he had a fall and broke his leg. He never walked again.

From London, the entourage, strapping the boss to a stretcher for the journey, flew to Freeport on Grand Bahama Island. They took the penthouse suite at the Xanadu Hotel owned by wealthy shipping magnate, Daniel K Ludwig. Hughes liked the place, though how he could tell one darkened room from another was a puzzle to those who knew him. To ensure peace and quiet he bought the hotel outright. He no longer watched television, so he no longer knew what day, month or season it was. His main amusement was watching films, especially those packed with action. His favourite was *Ice Station Zebra*, the story of a US–Soviet confrontation at the North Pole. He saw it at least 150 times. When he felt in good spirits he sang old jazz favourites in a cracked voice.

At the Xanadu, Hughes began to avoid eating again, and his weight fell off drastically. He was seventy years old on Christmas Eve, 1975, but his birthday and Christmas passed without observance.

At the beginning of 1976 he began to talk about moving again. This time he wanted to go to Acapulco, playground of the rich in Mexico. Nothing could have been more bizarre than the contrast between the emaciated figure, strapped to a stretcher, that was delivered secretly to the 20th floor of the Acapulco Princess Hotel, and the glorious brown bodies that lay toasting in the sun on the beaches below.

Hughes' physical appearance was now horrifying. Two of his aides, Melvin Stewart and Gordon Margulis, broke the ring of secrecy around the recluse by showing a picture of his emaciated body and talking to journalist James Phelam. Hughes had, apparently, shrunk to a cadaverous 90lbs; his former 6ft 4in frame had shrunk by three inches and he stood with a pronounced stoop. His hair and beard had grown to waist length again, his finger nails were two inches long and his toe nails curled over and over like yellow corkscrews. Doctors were appalled, and concluded Hughes had wrecked his health through drugs and malnutrition.

Howard Hughes died on the plane taking him back home to Houston, Texas, where it was hoped one last effort could be made to save him. His belongings were left in a pitiful pile in a corner of the darkened hotel room. They would not have filled one suitcase. For the funeral, his relatives had to buy a decent dark suit for him to be buried in. It was almost impossible to believe he had been one of the richest men ever in America.

Hetty Green

An old-fashioned black dress, threadbare, and turning a peculiar shade of green was, at one time, the only outer garment that Hetty Green possessed. It was never washed, in case it fell apart. Her only concession to wind and weather was a tatty old shawl or an umbrella as disreputable as the dress. It wasn't as though she couldn't afford a new one. At a time when the average American income per annum was $490, hers was more in the region of seven million.

At the turn of this century, the formidable Hetty became known as 'The Witch of Wall Street', a dealer who put the fear of God into the strongest man. Even J P Morgan, the arrogant, fearless banker, was so dismayed when he saw her coming that he used to scuttle across to the other side of the street or hide in a doorway.

Talking to Hetty was something of an ordeal. For one thing, she stank to high heaven. Her underclothes were never changed until they fell to pieces, and bathing was something that only other people did. Her capacious, shabby handbag was always stuffed full with scraps and cheap broken biscuits bought from a corner store so that she need never buy a meal in a restaurant.

One day Edward Hatch, director of Lord and Taylor's department store, found her scavenging through the contents of a Fifth Avenue rubbish bin. She looked so dreadful that he told her if she would call at the store some time he would be pleased to give her a really fine shawl from stock. Next day, there was a great commotion in the ladies' department of Lord and Taylor's. Hatch was informed that Hetty Green was raising hell with the

53

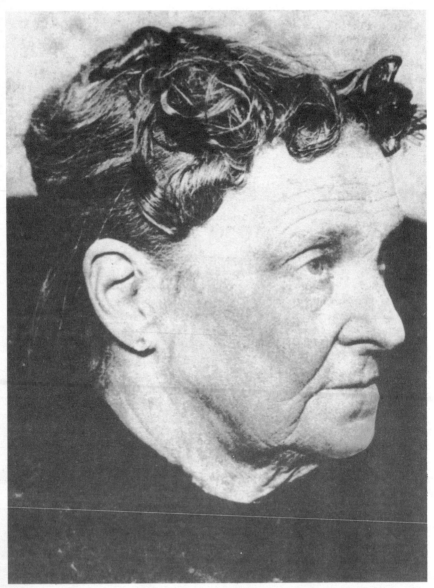

Hetty Green looked more like a tramp than a millionairess.

staff and claiming she'd been promised a shawl for free. The famous store keeper saw to it that his promise was kept; whereupon Hetty, sensing she was on to a good thing, asked if he had any damaged merchandize in the skirt line that she might have at a cheaper price. She went away with several items from old stock at 50 cents each. It was the first time she had bought anything for years. Afterwards, Hetty told everyone that Lord and Taylor's was a fine place to shop and her favourite outfitter.

Hetty's fortune came from the 19th-century days of whaling. She was born Hetty Howland Robinson on 21 November 1835, at New Bedford, Massachusetts; a great disappointment to her father who had looked forward to passing on his millions to a boy and founding a dynasty.

Hetty won her father over. By the age of six, she was reading the financial pages in the daily papers and enjoyed sitting on his knee and listening to him quote from the stock market report. When he died he left her a fortune worth $6 million in liquid assets.

Hetty was quite a handsome woman in her prime with a good figure, a peach-coloured complexion and ice-blue eyes. Edward Henry Green, member of a wealthy Vermont family, fell in love with her and proposed. Before she would permit the minister to marry them she made Green sign an agreement stating that, though man and wife in the sight of God, they were to keep separate accounts at the bank. There was to be no nonsense about common access to the safe deposit box. Hetty had no intention of letting her husband get his hands on her money.

Though not particularly maternal, she had two children by Edward Green: a son, Ned and a daughter, Sylvia. She soon tired of domesticity, however. She quarrelled with her in-laws and had pitched battles with every shopkeeper in the neighbourhood. Her only real interest was money and how to increase it by investment.

When her marriage ended after 14 years, Hetty moved into a shabby furnished apartment in a seedy part of Brooklyn, taking her two unfortunate children with her. She was genuinely fond of them, but saw no necessity to provide them with any home comforts. The heat was never turned on even in the coldest weather, and she said there was nothing wrong with cold water for washing and bathing. Personally, she didn't have time for such things.

The moment had come for her to descend on Wall Street. The New York Stock Exchange had hitherto been a closely guarded male preserve, but she had every intention of changing all that. She made her headquarters at the Seaboard National Bank, where she was given a desk in the foyer. Her business appeared to be conducted from a pile of cheap trunks and suitcases strewn about on the floor. Dealing with her was a pretty grim affair. 'She was feared and hated, and left many hitherto ruthless men scarred and bleeding on the financial battlefield,' wrote Lucius Beebe.

She went from one unsavoury lodging to another, dragging her children with her. All she did with her money was hoard it. She never spent a cent unless she had to, and her economies were pathetic. She did her own cooking on a gas ring and only bought the cheapest food available. She bought Graham Crackers by the barrel to save the grocer's profit, then lived off them for months on end. After reading the morning papers she would send her son out to re-sell them.

More serious than any of this was her miserliness about paying doctors. When Ned dislocated his knee falling off a sledge, she refused at first to get medical attention, saying the leg would right itself. When it became obvious that nothing of the kind was going to happen, she dressed him in ragged clothes so that he could get free treatment at the pauper's hospital. By the time a doctor got a chance to look at the dislocated knee, things had gone very wrong indeed. Ned had to have his leg amputated. It turned him against his mother.

Once her children had left home, Hetty moved into two shabby furnished rooms on the fifth floor of an apartment house. She still went to the bank most days but now travelled in some style. She had acquired a carriage that had been considered too derelict for anything but a henhouse. It didn't last long and caused great hilarity behind her back.

As she grew older, she became even more formidable. She still tried to dominate her children, but both had got away from her. Ned, with his cork leg, had started a colourful public career. Away from his mother he lived lavishly, running up enormous bills. Sylvia, a rather pathetic, drab young woman who wore outmoded clothes, had difficulty finding boyfriends – her mother considered they were all after her fortune and put them off. But she eventually became Sylvia Wilks, her husband having promised Hetty he would waive all rights to her property and money.

With age, and as her fortune grew bigger and bigger, Hetty became obsessed with the fear that she was being followed. Robbers and kidnappers were everywhere, and going to and from the bank she would take circuitous routes, double back on her tracks or even hide in doorways.

In 1916, after a violent argument with the housekeeper in the home of a friend, she suffered a stroke. Hetty had accused the woman of bankrupting her employer by using whole milk when skimmed milk would do just as well. She was told to mind her own business and reacted with a fit of temper. A blood vessel burst and one side of her was paralysed.

When Ned Green heard what had happened, he took charge of events. Doctors were sent for, and nurses were hired to look after her. But they were not allowed to appear at Hetty's bedside in uniform. Trained nurses got as much as $1 an hour and Ned knew the thought of the expense would give his mother another stroke.

She died in 1916, aged eighty, one of the richest women in the world. Nobody knew for sure exactly how much she was worth, but in Wall Street they hazarded a guess at well over $100 million. Had she known that a great deal of it was to be dissipated by her large, promiscuous son, 'Colonel' Ned Green, she would have turned in her grave. As though to wipe out the memory of all the mean years, he turned into one of the world's biggest spenders. Even his chamber pots were studded with diamonds!

J. Paul Getty

Though he was acclaimed as the world's richest man, J. Paul Getty was impoverished in almost every way, apart from his money. Married five times, every marriage ended in divorce. His four older sons stood aloof in awe of him, some in fear. His youngest child, Timmy, a pathetic waif who died when he was only twelve, hardly knew him. His last years were darkened by family tragedies. Countless mistresses and women friends adored him, but almost every romantic relationship was overshadowed by financial considerations. 'He never had a solid, loving relationship with anyone,' said one of his sons; and an aristocratic beauty with whom he *did* fall in love concluded, 'Money was a curse on him, the idea that distorted everything he did.'

Towards the end of his life, Getty lived at Sutton Place, a great Elizabethan manor deep in the English countryside, surrounded by a harem of beauties, all wondering what he would leave them. Strange stories leaked out and confirmed the legend that had been building up for years – of a billionaire with an incurable mean streak. After complaining about his telephone bills, he had had a pay phone installed in the hall at Sutton Place so that guests could pay for their own calls. He had developed a habit of pointedly locking up the Getty silver after dinner as soon as the last drops of port had been drunk. And when the weather was bitterly cold, instead

57

J. Paul Getty at home in Sutton Place with a bevy of beauties.

of increasing the heating he advised visitors to put on thicker sweaters or keep on their top coats!

Glimpses of Getty walking in the grounds of Sutton Place showed a shrivelled man with a thin, lugubrious face and cold blue eyes. He had made his first million when he was twenty-four and now he looked worn out with all that life had brought him. Only the beautiful women friends, jostling for his favour, brought a wintry smile to his face.

Sutton Place, in the depths of Surrey, was a world away from where it all began. Jean Paul Getty was born on 15 December 1892 in Minneapolis, Minnesota, the son of a highly successful American attorney who became an equally successful oilman. As a boy, Paul loved the adventure stories of G. A. Henty, and his interest in the oil industry was kindled when his father first took him out on site and he caught a whiff of the drama and excitement of an oil strike.

At sixteen, he asked permission to spend the summer holidays working on his father's lease in Indian territory, close to the Kansas stateline. The older Getty agreed, provided his son started at the bottom as a 'roustabout', an oilfield labourer. He was to be paid a roustabout's wages of three dollars a day and told he could expect no special treatment.

During the next three years, Paul divided his time between college in California, the handsome mansion his parents had bought in Los Angeles and the Oklahoma oil fields. At first, life on an oil rig came as a shock to the young man brought up in a comfortable, religious home. At the end of his first shift, he could hardly drag himself to his cot in the bunkhouse and his hands were a mass of bloody blisters. But he never complained.

At this stage, he had no plans to devote his life to the oil business. His ambition was to be a diplomat or a writer, and to travel in Europe. Because of his respect for his father, George Getty, however, he gave in to parental pressure and agreed to try his hand at the oil business for a couple of years.

In September 1914, when he was twenty-two, he set himself up as a 'wildcatter' in Tulsa and scoured the countryside for a promising parcel of land. He drove a battered old Model T Ford and often spent the night on the back seat. When he started drilling, however, he found he had inherited his father's luck. On his first 500-dollar site, the oil started coming in at the rate of 700 barrels a day.

A rapid succession of profitable transactions and new oil strikes followed. Soon he was president of his own company and went on to make more money than his father had even dreamed of. By the age of twenty-four he was a millionaire in his own right.

Few could have guessed from his appearance that, besides being an oilman of genius, Getty was also a legendary womanizer. Tall, well built, his sandy hair plastered down to control the curls, he was always soberly dressed, quiet and courteous., Only his light blue eyes, which could be as cold as ice or fiercely mocking, gave a hint of hidden passion.

Throughout his 20's, he devoted a great deal of time and energy to sex. Still living at his parents' house, he became adept at sneaking girls in and out of his private quarters. One of these, a girl called Elsie Eckctrom, had a baby and named Getty as her seducer. Although he denied the charge emphatically, the Press coverage of the case was sensational and brought him his first taste of notoriety.

By the age of thirty-one, Getty had gained a reputation as a playboy. He decided it was time he married and produced an heir. His choice was a beautiful young brunette, Jeanette Dumont, whose parents were Polish. She was just eighteen, barely out of school, and Getty persuaded her to elope with him to forestall parental objections. They were married at Ventura, California, on 1 October 1923.

Getty had no intention of allowing matrimony to interfere with business. He was often away from his young wife, and she protested, 'I married *you*, not your oil wells.' She gave him his first son, George Franklin Getty II, but within less than two years of their marriage she was filing for divorce. She accused her husband of carrying on with other women, of treating her with indifference and sometimes subjecting her to physical intimidation. He replied by accusing her of lying.

In the summer of 1926, after an acrimonious divorce, Getty left Los Angeles planning to enter the oil business in Mexico. Within a few months, he had come under the spell of Mexico itself – and another young girl. She was Allene Ashby, the beautiful, vivacious daughter of a wealthy and respectable Texas rancher.

Allene was just seventeen, the summer was hot and the mood romantic. He whisked her from under her father's nose and they were secretly married in the Mexican village of Cuernavaca on 27 October 1926. Within a few weeks they realized they had made a mistake. They had nothing in common and mutually agreed to draw a veil over the whole experience. Allene promised to seek a divorce as soon as she could, and swore her sister, Belle, to eternal silence.

The following June, Getty took a trip to Europe with his elderly parents. When they returned to America he stayed on, rented a bachelor pad in Paris and set out to enjoy himself. Staying at the Grand Hotel, Vienna, in the summer of 1928 he met a tall, ravishing, flaxen-haired blonde, called Adolphine Helmle, from Karlsruhe in Germany. She was a fresh, innocent eighteen-year-old, who had just finished a convent education and was travelling with her parents. 'Fini' proved irresistible. Getty followed the family around Europe, finally asking the flattered and overwhelmed girl to marry him at a clandestine meeting in Venice. Her father, Dr Otto Helmle, was not impressed by the rich, thirty-five-year-old American who had been married before, but he gave in. Fini became Mrs J P Getty III in Havana, Cuba, at the end of the the year.

Getty took his bride back to America and, once again, became completely engrossed in the oil business. He left the house early every day, returned late and often spent the evenings discussing business affairs with his father. Fini felt miserable and neglected, and when Getty showed little interest in her pregnancy, went home to Karlsruhe to have her baby alone. Getty chased after her, but was met with a frosty reception by her family. Though he did not want to lose her, especially after their son, Ronald, was born, the forceful Dr Helmle, convinced he could not make his daughter happy, pressed for divorce. He finally won his daughter round, and in November 1930 divorce proceedings began.

Even while trying to convince Fini's father that he loved his daughter he was consoling himself with a pretty office clerk, twenty-three-year-old Hildegard Kuhn, he met at a dance hall in Berlin. She was to have a continuing relationship with him for the next 46 years.

Getty's relationships with women paled to insignificance when he received a telegram saying that his father was dying. He admired and revered the old man more than any other human being, and wrote in his diary as he slipped away, 'No words can portray my mental anguish and feeling of helplessness.'

All the greater then the shock when George Getty's will was read. Paul learned that he had more or less been disinherited. He was to receive nothing but $500 000, money he neither needed nor wanted. What he had expected was control of the family business. His mother, Sarah, believed the snub was because the old man had been angry about his son's divorces; he had intended to alter the will, but somehow had never got round to it. The stage was set for a prolonged business struggle between mother and son. Eventually, he was elected President, Treasurer and General Manager of George F Getty Inc.; but complete authority rested with the majority stockholder – his mother.

Paul's position was not helped by the shambles of his private life. While his wife and baby son remained in Germany awaiting divorce proceedings, he had become involved with a young actress called Ann Rork, daughter of Hollywood producer, Sam Rork. He had first met and dated her seven years previously, when she was fourteen, but her father had whisked her away. Now twenty-one, she fell in love with him completely – 'I thought he was God' – she told her friends.

It was a very unorthodox wedding ceremony. Paul conveniently forgot that he was legally still married to Fini. There were just the two of them present. 'Do you want to marry me?' asked Paul. 'Yes,' answered Ann. 'We are married then,' said Paul. 'We don't need any third person to say things over us.'

Sarah Getty, who had been fond of the lovely German girl, refused to meet Ann Rork.

Beautiful women were never allowed to stand in the way of Getty's driving ambition for power in the oil industry. Ann, who gave birth to Jean Paul Getty II, was no exception. He took time off to marry her legally when his divorce came through but, as he was engaged in some of the most complex and important financial moves of his life, Ann and the new baby were completely forgotten. On 30 December 1933, she gave birth to Getty's fourth son, Gordon. He hardly noticed.

The marriage lasted just over two years. At the end of 1934, Ann filed for divorce alleging 'extreme cruelty' and painted a dismal picture of life with her rich husband. Getty went home to live with his mother. A fourth broken marriage did not seem to upset him unduly; what did concern him was the appalling publicity he received. He fled Los Angeles when the court case was over, and then stayed in New York, where he tried to obliterate his image as a terrible husband by becoming a man of culture. Indulging his newly developed taste for art and antiques, he proceeded to build up an art collection. Prices were low because of the depression and his 'bargains' later became priceless.

Getty's pursuit of art was combined with the pursuit of an auburn-haired, twenty-two-year-old nightclub singer, Louise 'Teddy' Lynch, niece of Bernard Baruch, the multi-millionaire financier. Getty sat night after night at the Stork Club where she performed, never taking his eyes off her, then sending flowers and champagne to her dressing-room. At the age of forty-three, he proposed marriage for the fifth time.

Teddy Lynch was a strong-willed, temperamental girl, and quite a match for him. She joined him in Europe, where he was busy hunting for antiques, and they were married in Rome on 14 November 1939. However, when Getty sailed back to New York, she decided to stay there and continue her singing lessons. They did not meet again until Teddy managed to get a crossing in June 1942. They had a passionate, delayed honeymoon, and it looked as though he had met the right woman at last. He became a father for the fifth time on 15 June 1946 when Teddy gave birth to a son, Timmy, prematurely. It was noted that three weeks passed before Getty managed to get to see them.

After the death of his mother, Getty set out to build a worldwide oil empire. In order to do this, he needed to spend time in Europe. It was only meant to be a temporary measure but throughout the '50s he wandered around from capital to capital like a nomad, always staying in the top hotels, driving thousands of miles in his Cadillac. He took his business papers and files with him in cardboard boxes, and from these increasingly battered containers he controlled his worldwide interests. A wardrobe of clothes was kept in the basement of each hotel he stayed in, ready for when he passed that way again.

Getty did not regard his marriage to Teddy as a serious tie. When he was away from her – most of the time – he travelled with other women friends. By 1955, Teddy had not seen Getty for four years. She sailed to England with their son, Timmy, to try to persuade him to return to America and make a home for them all. Freckle-faced Timmy had had an operation for a tumour on the optic nerve and was in delicate health, but Getty refused to go back to the States. The truth was he was beginning to have a serious phobia about crossing the Atlantic by boat or plane, fearing he would die in an accident. Though he always intended to go home again, he never did. On 3 January 1956, the fifth Mrs Getty reluctantly filed for divorce, citing her husband's refusal to return from Europe as a sure sign that the marriage was over.

Strangely enough, Getty remained on friendly terms with several of the wives who had taken him to court in anger. But his relationship with his sons was far more damaging. He spent hardly any time with them and treated them coldly. His oldest son, George, born to his first wife, Jeanette, had seen so little of him that he once called him 'Mr Getty' when they met. He was an intelligent man who suffered deeply from a feeling of insecurity, almost certainly caused by his father's neglect. Ronald, the son of Getty's second wife, Fini, hid his feelings with a certain arrogance and bore the emotional scar of being unfairly treated financially. J Paul Getty Jnr., the son of fourth wife, Ann, and Getty's favourite, was good-looking, charming and artistic. He was taken into the firm but had no idea what rôle he was supposed to play, and by the mid 1960s, Paul had fired him from his post as Director of Getty Oil in Italy, blaming him for a two-million-dollar annual loss. It was only Gordon, also Ann's child, who had been ignored by his father, who in the end faced up to him. Mostly, though, the sons were all awkward and uncomfortable in their father's presence. Getty, on the other hand, thought himself a good father and wept when his youngest son Timmy died at the age of twelve.

After twelve years of wandering around Europe, Getty finally decided to settle in England, and in 1959 he bought Sutton Place from the Duke of Sutherland. Visitors found the place cold and dreary, more like a museum than a home, with its massive oak doors, grilles on the windows and fierce guard dogs roaming the grounds. Getty seemed afraid to be alone, and surrounded himself with adoring women friends who vied with each other for his attention. As he got older, he worried about his virility and took pills as well as injections to increase his libido.

His meanness became legendary. On one occasion Lady Diana Cooper, the famous English beauty, was his guest. She complained of rheumatism and Getty told her he had a first class remedy and would send it to her. Several days later, she received a used tube of Bengue's Balsam, the neck of the tube bent over so that she could squeeze out the last drop.

Three terrible tragedies hit the Getty family in the early 1970s. His third son and namesake, Paul Jnr., had married jet-set beauty Talitha Pol against his father's wishes. On the morning of 11 July 1971 she was found dying from a massive overdose of heroin. Paul Jnr. was so shocked that he became a recluse. He never saw his father again.

The second tragedy came when George, Getty's heir apparent, worried about maintaining his position in the business world, took an overdose on 6 June 1973 and was found unconscious in his apartment in California. When told of his death, Getty sat rigid in a chair for half an hour, not speaking, just staring in front of him. He had never once given George credit for what he had achieved.

About a month after George's death, Paul's grandson, Paul Getty III was kidnapped and taken to a lonely house in the bleak, stony mountain district of Calabria. A vast ransom was demanded, and when it was not immediately forthcoming, the kidnappers cut off one of the boy's ears. During the six months young Paul was in captivity, his grandfather did little to secure his grandson's release.

Towards the end of his life Getty began to tire of the women vying for his attention. There were nine of them in all, drifting in and out, listening to his memories. For years he had tantalized everyone with hints of what they could expect from his will. Now he used this ploy more than ever.

Paul Getty had a terrible fear of death. When he developed cancer of the prostate gland he refused to go into hospital, nor would he go upstairs to bed. He said he wanted to die with his boots on. So, an electrically operated chair was installed in his study that let down into a bed.

J Paul Getty died peacefully, sitting in his favourite armchair at Sutton Place on 6 June 1976. Two days later, his coffin of English oak was loaded aboard a TWA flight bound for Los Angeles. He had left the bulk of his fortune to the Getty Museum in Malibu, California, which housed his great collection of paintings and antiquities. But there were still enough millions to go round; enough to make the Getty clan rich for generations to come.

Chapter Three

YOU WIN SOME, YOU LOSE SOME

Fortunes that are made, enjoyed,
then lost, leaving their victims
a shadow of their former selves.

'Never ask of money spent,
Where the spender thinks it went.
Nobody was ever meant,
To remember or invent,
What he did with every cent.'

Robert Frost (1936)

Queen Soraya

Two moments were unforgettable in the life of Soraya Esfandiary. One was when she stood by the side of His Imperial Majesty the Shah of Iran at the age of eighteen and became his Empress. The other was the day she stood on the steps of the plane taking her to Europe and out of his life for ever.

Only seven years stretched between the joy of the first and the anguish of the second; seven years at the end of which she lost the man she loved, her country and her crown. And all for one reason alone – she could not give the Shah the son and heir he wanted.

The story of Queen Soraya and the Shah is one of the most poignant in modern history. Everyone presumed the marriage to be one of convenience. Everything depended on whether she could provide an heir for the Peacock Throne. What no one had taken into account was the fact that the two people concerned would fall deeply in love.

Soraya, a ravishingly beautiful young woman, was the daughter of an Iranian father and a German mother. She had silky raven-black hair, high cheekbones, huge, dreamy green eyes and full red lips. Only a fraction of that beauty was evident when, one day in 1950, the Shah saw some rather fuzzy snapshots of her taken in St Moritz. But they were enough to rouse his interest.

Officials at the Iranian court had begun to despair of the Shah ever taking serious interest in what they considered to be a marriageable girl. None of the aristocratic young women they paraded before him at receptions and balls seemed to have touched his heart. Mohammed Reza Pahlevi was now thirty-one years old, imperiously handsome, a fine sportsman and fabulously rich. But he was also a lonely and unhappy man. His first marriage to Princess Fawzia, sister of King Farouk of Egypt, had ended in divorce. Their only child was a daughter, Princess Shahnaz. He knew it was his duty to marry again to secure the Pahlevi dynasty, but he was modern in his thinking and wanted to do so, if possible, for love.

He was sitting alone one night when one of his mother's ladies-in-waiting, and an old friend of the royal family, showed him pictures of her niece on the ski slopes in Switzerland. She told him her name was Soraya. 'She seems very pretty,' he admitted. 'What a pity the photographs are not

The beautiful Soraya Esfandiary – Queen Soraya.

clearer.' His obvious interest stirred her to action. She telephoned to London, where Soraya was studying, and ordered more pictures to be taken immediately and sent to her at the palace in Tehran.

A few days later, the Shah was presented with clear pictures of the stunning eighteen-year-old girl, laughing among the gold-tinted autumn leaves in St James's Park, London. There was also a studio portrait, serious, dignified, showing the beauty of her slightly oriental features. He studied her face carefully; then said, with a laugh, 'Well, perhaps this is the one . . .' There was a bustle among the rather formidable women in the Shah's family. His mother, the Dowager Empress, told her daughter, Princess Shams: 'Fly to London and have a look at this girl.'

Soraya Esfandiary was the daughter of a Persian diplomat and his German-born wife. Her father, Khalil Esfandiary, belonged to the clan of the Baktiari, feuding nomads whose ancestry could be traced back to the 12th century. Soraya was born at Isfahan on 22 June 1932, spent part of her childhood in Europe but returned to her birthplace during the Second World War. Once hostilities were over, her mother sent her to finishing schools in Switzerland so that she could absorb the European tradition rather than that of the submissive female behind the veil. She loved Switzerland and considered the years she spent at school there among the happiest in her life.

She was already receiving proposals of marriage. All the suitors came from old Iranian families who visited her parents at their house in Zurich and asked for her hand. She was told not to take the proposals too seriously; her studies came first. To emphasize the point, she was sent to London in the summer of 1950 to perfect her English.

That autumn her cousin, Gudars Baktiari, who was studying at the same language school, asked her if he could take photographs of her. They were, he said, for his mother to show to the Dowager Empress. She was intrigued and puzzled. When her father wrote to say the Shah had asked for her to be presented at court, she began to have premonitions that her life was about to change.

Premonition turned to certainty when the Shah's eldest sister, Princess Shams, arrived in London, took her to dinner at the Iranian Embassy and suggested they flew to Paris together to do some shopping. But the visit to Paris turned out to be far more than a simple shopping expedition. Soraya was schooled in some of the formal protocol and etiquette demanded at court in Tehran. She was taking her first steps towards ascending the Peacock Throne.

Accompanied by her father and Princess Shams, Soraya took the night flight to Tehran on 7 October. She had scarcely unpacked her suitcase when a call came through from the palace: the Dowager Empress had arranged a small dinner at which only the innermost family circle would be present. Though she was tired, she slipped into one of her new Paris dresses and made herself ready.

The formidable old lady was waiting for her, seated in a deep chair covered in yellow silk. Members of the Royal Family were grouped around her. They welcomed her amiably and for 15 minutes questioned her lengthily about her health and the health of her relatives, a mark of good manners in Iranian society.

A servant entered the room and announced: 'His Majesty the Shah!'

The Shah was strikingly handsome in the dress uniform of a general of the Iranian Air Force. Soraya trembled a little when she was presented to him, but managed to bow with dignity. Rather stiffly, he led her to the dining table and beckoned her to sit next to him. Throughout the meal he gave her his whole attention, questioning her about her studies in Switzerland and England. He, too, had been to boarding school in Switzerland and knew the country around Montreux and Lausanne. As the evening went on, the strong attraction between the two of them began to be very noticeable.

As they left the palace Soraya's father asked her: 'Well, what do you think of him?'

'I like him,' she replied.

'Are you willing to marry him?'

'Do I have to make up my mind at once?'

'It would be better,' her father replied. 'The Shah requested just now that I ask you for your answer this evening.'

This was all hastier than she had expected. But in her autobiography, Soraya says: 'My sensation of pleasure did not leave room either for surprise or confusion . . . without a second's hesitation I agreed to marry him.'

Next morning her photograph was in the world's newspapers. Three days later, the official celebrations to mark their engagement took place in the Imperial Palace. The wedding was announced for 27 December.

Every day for the next three weeks the young couple went horse riding, driving into the country for picnics and flying in the Shah's private plane. By the end of October, however, Tehran was in the grip of a typhoid epidemic. Soraya returned from one of her outings with a high colour, abnormally bright eyes and her body shaking with fever. The court doctor was called and confirmed that she, too, was a victim.

For days her temperature raged around 106 degrees and her life hung by a thread. When the crisis had passed she was confined to bed for three months as she fought her way back to health and strength. It was during this period that Soraya and the Shah fell deeply in love. Each day he spent hours at her bedside; he brought her flowers and gifts and, when she began to feel better, had a record player and a film projector fixed up in her room. He was tender and kind and now she *really* knew she wanted to marry him.

The wedding had been postponed until 12 February 1951. Soraya was still weak, and when the great day dawned and she woke to find Tehran in deep snow, the doctor insisted she wore thick white woollen stockings underneath her wedding dress. And what a dress! Designed by Christian Dior it was a breathtaking creation of silver brocade, tulle and floating ostrich feathers. The train was 12 yards long and the whole concoction weighed 40 lbs. During the ceremony Soraya nearly fainted. The Shah saw her distress and after the ceremony asked a lady-in-waiting to cut away part of the incredible skirt to lessen the weight. It was so full that nobody even noticed.

At the great reception that night Soraya wore some of the Pahlevi Crown Jewels for the first time. Her tiara sparkled with diamonds; round her neck were rows of emeralds; great emerald drops hung from her ears and one flawless green jewel on her finger caught the light. Everyone was talking about the wedding presents. The Russian dictator, Stalin, had sent the Shah a writing set studded with black diamonds, and for Soraya there was a snow white Russian mink coat.

After a two-week honeymoon in a villa on the shores of the Caspian Sea, the couple were forced to return to Tehran where a political crisis threatened. They had only been back three days when the Prime Minister of Iran was shot by fanatics while attending divine service in a mosque. His place was taken by Dr Mohamed Mossadeq, a virulent anti-monarchist whose ambition was to make himself dictator. The antics of this dangerous, emotionally unstable man threw Iran into chaos for the next two-and-a-half years and involved the Shah in a bitter row with Britain over the supply of Iranian oil.

Under the influence of Mossadeq, Iran slid towards ruin and anarchy. The situation became so dangerous as Mossadeq's hysterical supporters yelled for the execution of the entire royal family, that in August 1953 the Shah and Soraya fled to Rome. Mossadeq was finally ousted by the loyal General Zahedi who gathered the support of the army. Once the situation had settled down, the royal couple returned to a jubilant welcome from the Iranian people.

Trouble had brought the Shah and Soraya to an even deeper understanding. After the Mossadeq crisis there were to be others, equally frightening. Iran was in a constant state of ferment, but there followed a period in which the royal couple were able to settle down to a more regular married life, to carry out their various social duties and to visit ordinary Iranians in their villages and homes.

Both the Shah and Soraya loved sports. They swam, rode and sailed together, played volley-ball and learned to water ski. Like any other young couple they enjoyed parties, fancy dress balls, private film shows and picnics. Late in 1954 they set out on a series of state visits to Britain, Germany and the United States. Everywhere, Soraya was admired and photographed, and everywhere people were asking the same question: when was she going to give the Shah the son and heir he desperately needed?

There could be no official coronation of the Empress until a Crown Prince had been born. After four years of marriage, the cradle remained empty. To show his faith in her, Mohammad Reza told Soraya that he intended to have a crown specially designed for his Empress. One day he took her to the Melli Bank, the national bank where the crown jewels are kept, and helped her to choose the precious stones to go in it.

Soraya comforted herself with the thought that her own mother had to wait six years for her arrival. Doctors she consulted assured her that it was quite possible that this kind of thing ran in families. She must be patient. Worry would only make matters worse.

But the Shah, ruling over such a volatile country and with many jealous and ambitious men around him, could not afford to wait. At thirty-five, after 15 years and two marriages, he still had no heir to the throne. He gently suggested to his Queen that they should both undergo medical examinations. She agreed, and on 8 December 1954 they were booked into the Presbyterian Medical Center in New York. For three days they were both given a thorough check-up. All tests proved that they were perfectly normal. The doctors saw no reason why they should not have children. Queen Soraya was told to go home and be patient.

For some time the Shah did not refer to the subject of his heir. They threw themselves into good works and charitable causes hoping the problem would resolve itself. On 3 April 1957, he appointed a new Prime Minister, Dr Manachur Eghbal, a university professor of whom great things were expected. He was full of new ideas.

A few days after his appointment, Dr Eghbal asked for an audience with the Shah. He spoke quietly but firmly: 'Your Majesty, if I am to undertake reform in your name, your own authority must be unassailable. Either the Empress must present you with an heir in the near future, or the dynasty's future must be assured in some other way.'

Soraya, by this time, had given up hope. She knew that if she was to hold on to her marriage, she would have to suggest a solution. At first she thought of Princess Shahnaz, the Shah's daughter. Could she be nominated Crown Princess? There was also the possibility of choosing one of the Shah's half-brothers.

Haggard and distraught at the thought of losing her, the Shah decided to call his Council of Wise Men together to discuss what could be done. He advised Soraya to await the outcome of discussions, which were held in Europe so that she would not be around to be hurt. She agreed to go skiing at St Moritz.

Thus, on 13th February 1958, almost seven years to the day since their wedding, Queen Soraya kissed her husband goodbye, walked through a guard of honour to the waiting plane and turned for one last look. They were never to meet again.

Day after day, Soraya waited in Switzerland to see what the outcome of the Wise Men's discussion would be. She spoke to the Shah on the telephone, but it was no consolation. He sounded so forlorn. After a month, three emissaries from Tehran arrived to see her. The only glimmer of hope they gave her was that she could remain Empress if she agreed to the Shah taking a second wife who would give him an heir. He was entitled to do this under Islamic law. Would she agree? Soraya gazed at the three anxious faces, her eyes filled with tears and she shook her head.

A few days later the Shah announced the divorce 'with great sorrow'. There was no doubting the Shah's grief. He looked as if his heart was breaking. Soraya, inconsolable for a time, threw herself madly into the mainstream of jet-set life. She was seen with film stars and playboys, her name was linked with princes and millionaires. She was always on the move and never seemed to smile. She would never speak of the past.

Eighteen months after they had parted, the Shah married Farah Diba and she gave him the heir he longed for. But as fate would have it, they, too, eventually were forced into a bitter exile when the Ayatollah overthrew the Shah, leaving the Peacock Throne unoccupied.

Nina Dyer

Nina Dyer was not a raving beauty. She was a quiet, withdrawn, enigmatic young woman who earned her living as a not very successful model. But, within the space of a few years, she married *two* world famous millionaires. One made her a baroness, the other, a princess. Between them they showered her with jewels and bought her spectacular presents. Other women could only look on and wonder.

Somewhere, something went wrong with what appeared to be idyllic romances. The first marriage lasted ten months, the second, three years. She spent the last years of her life as a lonely divorcee, drifting from one glittering party to another. Suddenly, the presents didn't matter to her any more. 'It reaches a point where a woman loved by a rich man only has to admire something in passing and it arrives on her doorstep, tied with blue ribbons,' she said in a voice of disillusion.

When Nina Dyer first started out as a model, the attractive, gregarious girls who worked with her felt she was not one of them, that she was not interested in casually dating young Mayfair men but was saving herself for someone special. The fact that she had been brought up in Ceylon, now Sri Lanka, made her 'different'. Born on 15 February 1930 she had always presumed her father to be Ceylon tea planter, Stanley Dyer, with whom her mother lived until she died in 1954. Years later William Aldrich, director of an electrical firm in Chaldon, Surrey, her mother's real husband, claimed Nina was his child.

Brought back to England, she became a drama student at Mrs Helen Ackerley's school of Speech, Drama and Deportment, in Liverpool. When she had finished the course Mrs Ackerley told her the brutal truth: that she would never make an actress. She advised her, instead, to try modelling.

Nina was a striking looking girl with dark titian hair and a slender figure, but her features were too bold for real beauty. At first she tried modelling in London, where she lived in a very modest flat in South Kensington. She did not make a great impression among the leggy beauties of the day, but suddenly decided to try her luck in Paris, found work with the couturiers and developed a new, better poised, more soigné look.

At every opportunity, she went off to the Riviera with a bikini and a pair of Pekingese dogs. Photographers soon began to notice her and her picture appeared frequently in the newspapers. On one such holiday, when she was twenty-two, she met and became romantically involved with Nicolas Franco, Spanish ambassador to Portugal and younger brother of the Spanish dictator. He offered to sponsor a film career for her in Spain, but she had other plans.

Back in Paris she had been taken up by rich and influential friends who took her to parties at some of the smartest homes in Paris. She now dressed superbly and attracted many admiring glances. One night, over the rim of a cocktail glass, her eyes met those of thirty-three-year-old Baron Heinrich von Thyssen, one of the richest men in Europe.

The blond Baron, who had inherited a steel and shipping fortune from his uncle, Fritz von Thyssen, one of Hitler's great supporters, was an extremely attractive proposition. Though still married to Austrian-born Princess Theresa de Lippe, divorce was on its way. He was now a naturalized Swiss and would soon be free to look for a companion among Europe's loveliest women.

Nina, with her slight lisp, Riviera suntan and silken poise intrigued him. Next day he telephoned. She saw no point in playing the old game of hard to get – 'From the minute he spoke to me, he was the only man in my life,' she said at the time. They were soon seen together at all the smart places. His first presents to her were two cars – a Ferrari sports and a Simca – both with gold ignition and door keys.

When they were eventually engaged, he gave her a £30 000 ring and a £20 000 brooch to match. They were married in Colombo, Ceylon, in December 1954. She was twenty-four. A Paris in Spring wedding had been planned, but when Nina's mother died in a road accident outside Colombo they decided to marry quietly at the island's register office. She wore a simple, low-necked white dress. He wore a shark-skin suit. And they looked very much in love.

Cruising in San San Bay off Jamaica on their honeymoon, they spotted an uninhabited, palm-fringed island with pure white sandy beaches. Nina turned to her husband, impulsively: 'Heini, I would *love* to live on that island!' Gazing into her lovely eyes he assured her, 'So you shall, my dear, so you shall.'

Thyssen bought Pellow Island for Nina without disclosing the cost. They planned to build a house there for holidays, decorating the rooms with French murals and installing an all-American modern kitchen.

He gave her so many spectacular presents. Among the jewels he bought was a necklace of huge black pearls and ear-rings and a black solitaire pearl ring to match. Wanting to give her a house of her own, he acquired the

Nina Dyer – she married two of the world's richest men.

Château Midori, 15 miles from Paris, where she started a small menagerie. Being an animal lover she was over the moon when he presented her with a three-month-old black panther and a baby leopard. To make them feel at home, she installed a huge tropical climbing plant with vine-like branches in the middle of her drawing room. It began to take over and creep across the ceiling.

They had only been married ten months when Nina announced that they were to part. Divorce proceedings were to be heard at Lugano, Switzerland, where the Baron had his home. 'What went wrong? The truth is we didn't really get on together from the start,' Thyssen admitted to his surprised friends. 'There are many reasons. Partly, I think, we married too hastily.' Nina complained, 'He set a pace few marriages could survive. He had so many business interests he was seldom in the same place or country for more than a few days at a time. It was all high finance and high society.'

Nina settled down to wait for her divorce in her rambling, half empty château in the French town of Garches. She had never got round to furnishing it and now asked for money to buy carpets and curtains. For company, she had a flock of pet parrots, 10 dogs, two humming birds, her panther and the leopard. When the parting finally came, 'Incompatibility' was given as the reason for the breakdown of the marriage. The Baron gave Nina £1 000 000 and his best wishes. After the divorce he went on to marry twenty-four-year-old beauty, Fiona Campbell-Walter, another London model.

Nina continued to hobnob with the titled rich of Europe. She got to know playboy Prince Aly Khan, then escorting the famous French model, Bettina. One night, Aly asked her to one of the champagne parties he always gave in Paris after the Grand Prix. He introduced her to his dark, handsome half-brother, Prince Sadruddin . . . and it was love at first sight for both of them.

At the time, it was thought that when the old Aga Khan died, twenty-four-year-old Sadruddin might become his successor as ruler of the Moslem Ismaelis. If that happened, his wife would become Begum. However, the Aga had already decided that his grandson, Karim, would take over on his death. Nevertheless, Sadruddin was a young man held in the highest esteem; he was more serious than Aly, more stable.

'Sadri', as everyone called him, was a student at Harvard. He was in Europe for a short time to see his father, who was ill. Since he was seventeen, his name had been linked with beautiful women, among them French ballerina, Ethery Pageva, French actress, Anouk, seventeen-year-old Princess Shahnaz, daughter of the Shah of Iran, and British socialite Doon Plunket, a member of the Guinness family. Now he began to woo Nina.

Unlike his brother, Aly, Sadri had no interest in racing but, like Nina, he loved animals. They also shared an interest in music and outdoor sports. She was fascinated by his hobby – collecting Persian miniatures of the 16th and 17th centuries. One thing pleased her: no one could accuse her of fortune hunting; Baron von Thyssen's divorce settlement meant she had a fortune in her own right.

After he had proposed, only one thing worried Prince Sadruddin. The Aga Khan had made it plain that he wanted this son to marry an Asiatic girl; he thought there was too much European blood in the family. Sadri took Nina to meet his mother first. Princess Andree Khan was delighted with his choice. Then he went alone to confront his father. Fortunately, the old Aga was satisfied with his son's choice, especially when he heard that Nina was prepared to become a Moslem.

Once it was known that Nina was about to marry her second millionaire, she was besieged for interviews. She denied being a schemer; she said nothing was further from the truth; luck just seemed to come her way without her doing anything about it: 'It has been like that during most of my grown up life.' Asked the secret of her success she sipped an orange juice and replied modestly: 'Be simple and dignified in your ways. Be natural. Be yourself. Don't put on airs. The very rich are often simple people with simple tastes.'

Nina and Prince Sadruddin were married in Geneva on a beautiful June day in 1957. She wore an exquisite short wedding dress of palest silver-grey organdie, designed by Dior. All her Thyssen jewels were left at home. Her ring was just a simple band of gold. Sadri wore one exactly the same. First a civil ceremony was performed by the Mayor. Then came the religious rites, in which two Imams officiated, at the Prince's magnificent château outside Geneva. The wedding was a strictly family affair with only 29 guests. Aly Khan was there with Bettina, and the bridesmaid was Sadri's young cousin. The bride changed her name to Princess Shirin, the word 'shirin' meaning sweetness.

For two years the marriage seemed to go well. The pair had made a touching pact on their wedding day, never to be seated apart at dinner tables or to dance with anyone else at receptions, balls and nightclubs. It was all the more noticeable, then, when they began to appear in public separately.

In material terms, Nina had scooped the pool again. The Prince had given her a £36 000 blue diamond ring, an expensive sports car and made her a £50 000 a year tax free allowance. She lived in superb style at their château in Switzerland and their villa in the south of France. But she was lonely a great deal of the time.

Sadri became immersed in a project to save the Nubian monuments, which were threatened with submersion when the Egyptians built the Aswan Dam. He became absorbed in the diplomatic world and, by October 1960, was in New York a great deal of the time as an ambassador to the United Nations. The two of them had not been seen together for months. Nina was thought to be living quietly on Capri.

They parted in 1960 and were divorced two years later. The cause of the rift was, again, incompatibility.

Nina went back to her home in France and tried to make a social life for herself. Every evening she dressed carefully, chose jewels from her fabulous collection and went out. Sometimes she gave lavish parties, but it was obvious that she was a very lonely woman. A Portuguese couple were her only servants and she became very fond of their child, spoiling him with sweets and toys.

She arrived home at midnight on 3 July 1965, talked with her housekeeper for a few minutes, then, smiling sweetly, wished her goodnight. When her breakfast tray was taken to her bedroom next morning there was no reply. Eventually, the door was broken down and Nina was found dead. There was an empty tube of sleeping pills, but no note.

Both husbands attended her funeral at Garches cemetery, only a few hundred yards from her home. They covered her grave with hundreds of red roses. There was a card from the Baron, which said simply: 'From Heini to Nina.'

She left a will asking that her money should be used for the care of animals, but the Swiss court, for reasons not given, ruled it invalid. That was when William Aldrich of Surrey came forward to claim that he was her father. Her wonderful jewels were auctioned in Geneva and among the buyers rumoured to be interested were names like Elizabeth Taylor, Sophia Loren, Jackie Onassis and Maria Callas.

Nina was only thirty-five when she died. She had shot from comparative obscurity to be the wife of two very rich men within a very short time. But there is an old adage which says: 'From rags to riches, from riches to emptiness.' Perhaps she found it had come true.

Vivian Nicholson

Vivian Nicholson, a Yorkshire lass who still lives in Castleford where she was born, is remembered by people all over the country for one thing: when her husband Keith was lucky enough to come up on the Pools in 1961 she made no secret about what she was going to do with the money. 'I'm going to spend, spend, spend!' she shouted, joyously.

Who could blame her? All her life she had been so poor, then, suddenly, she was standing beneath the bright lights in one of London's top hotels holding a cheque for £152 300 18s 6d. She couldn't believe there was so much money in the world. And outside, in the shop windows, were all the things she'd never been able to afford.

She was twenty-five when it happened, a brighty, perky blonde who had not had an easy time ever since she was born. Her father was a miner, but most of the time he was too ill to work. She went to the council school in Castleford and left when she was fifteen. Sometimes she day-dreamed about going to art school but, with five children in the family, it just wasn't possible. As the eldest, she had to go out to work and 'bring a bit in'. First she worked in a sweet factory, then in a flour mill. She didn't like either, but when a chance came to work in the local cinema, she thought it would be more exciting and became an usherette.

Vivian's first husband came along when she was twenty-three, but the marriage was not a success and she was divorced seven months later. Soon after, she met a dark-haired, pleasant faced young miner called Keith Nicholson. Though he was two years younger than she was, they hit it off immediately and their wedding took place in 1960.

They managed to get a council house in Kershaw Avenue, Airedale, near Castleford. Keith worked at nearby Wheldale Colliery and earned £14 a week. There was enough to get by on, but they often dreamed about what it would be like to win the Pools. Keith did them every Saturday, just a 4-shilling stake and no particular system. But one particular weekend in 1961, he felt a chill go up his spine as he checked the results on TV. He knew he had six draws, then seven, but he wasn't *sure* whether he had the magical eight. Vivian's father called round. He checked them and said he *knew* they had eight. They hardly dared look at each other.

79

Vivian Nicholson – 'I'm going to spend, spend, spend!'

The Pools representatives turned up on the following Monday. Both Vivian and Keith had had sleepless nights since the discovery, and even when they were told officially they couldn't take it in. They still didn't know how much they had won, though they were assured it would be a sum worth having. All depended on how many other people had filled in eight draws.

For the next few weeks they could hardly sleep or eat. They did not find out that they were the *only* winners until just before they caught the train to London for the presentation. When they got off at the other end, the Press was waiting. 'What are you going to do with the money?' shouted reporters. 'I'm going to spend, spend, spend!' she laughed back.

They stayed at the Grosvenor Hotel in Park Lane, had a memorable night out at the Pigalle and braced themselves for the presentation next day. Vivian had an idea that £75 000 was the most you could win on the Pools. When they told her the cheque was for more than £150 000, she felt as if the world had stopped turning.

While a bemused Keith tried to take in the advice that was being hurled at him by the finance men, Vivian went on her first shopping spree – to Harrods. She couldn't believe it was all real. Viv Nicholson from Castleford buying clothes for herself and the children, masses of toys, perfume, an 80-guinea watch – and buying them in the poshest store you could imagine! The hotel room was packed from floor to ceiling with Harrods parcels, and *still* it didn't seem *real*.

They flew back to Yorkshire feeling like film stars, with flash bulbs popping and the Press hanging on every word. Vivian, her arms full of flowers, was asked again and again if she'd really said she was going to 'Spend, spend, spend'. All she could think of was getting back home and giving the children their toys.

That first night in Castleford was wonderful. They threw open the doors and invited everyone in for a drink. When the house was full they drank outside in the garden, even on the pavement. That was a party they'd never forget. But next day was different. Envy started to creep in. Envy and resentment. Why should the Nicholsons have all the luck? They were young, and there were older people who deserved it more. When they walked into their local pub for a drink, people fell silent and moved away. 'If I sit and talk to you, people will say I'm after something,' one neighbour explained, curtly.

Now they were rich they could no longer stay in their council house. They bought a show house in Grange Avenue, Garforth, near Leeds . . . and regretted every minute they spent there. Vivian felt the chill as soon as she arrived. The neighbours, she said, ignored her; they would even cross

YOU WIN SOME, YOU LOSE SOME

the road to avoid speaking to her. She and her husband had been cold-shouldered out of Castleford because of the money; it was obvious they were not wanted here either.

Vivian found a way of getting her own back. After a night at the pub with Keith, she invited everybody back to the house for the loudest party she could manage. The record player was on full blast and everyone was laughing and singing. Inevitably, the police came. But when she encountered frosty stares next morning, she grinned to herself.

'We stayed there long enough for them to get really fed up with us and for us to really get mad and fed up with them,' Vivian told Stephen Smith and Peter Razzell, sociologists at London University who were conducting research on Pools winners. 'But they forced me into a lot of things; it isn't the Pools that change you, you know; it's the people around that change you,' she explained.

The couple found another house: a large bungalow on the Halbury Moor. It was expensive, but there was plenty of space for the children and their ponies, as well as all the cars they had bought – Vivian had six cars in four years, and Keith changed his every two months. She went to the most expensive department stores in Leeds, and furnished the house exactly as she wanted it. Her favourite purchases were a £1000 four-seater settee and an organ. She also bought herself a £1000 diamond solitaire ring and £600 worth of clothes to cheer herself up.

Once the two older children had been sent to boarding school, both Vivian and Keith began to get bored. They had some good foreign holidays, including a trip to America, but at home they drank too much just to fill in time. When Viv began to feel ill and worried about becoming an alcoholic, Keith started going out drinking without her.

Keith was spending money like water, but he wouldn't discuss financial affairs; he wouldn't even go to the bank when the manager asked to see him. He was convinced the money would go on for ever. He had taken up fishing, shooting and golf, buying the most expensive equipment available. After taking up racing, he bought three racehorses and obviously had plans to gradually build up a stable. But more than anything, Keith was mad about cars.

Whatever car he bought, he managed to smash it up within two months. He even had a crash on the way to his driving test. His latest car was a beautiful, shiny new Jaguar and he couldn't wait to get behind the wheel. One morning, he told Vivian he was going to see some new ponies for the children. His uncle was going along, too. He was dying to show him how the car performed. On the way back, he ran off the road. By the time ambulancemen got Keith out, he was dead.

Vivian began to drink again. She felt lost without Keith, and she suddenly realized they had spent an awful lot of money. She was advised to sell the bungalow and buy something cheaper. The cars had to go and the children could not stay at boarding school. By the time accountants had sorted out Viv's financial position, she found she had just £10 a week to live on; but she fought like a tigress to get a lump sum from the remaining money in Keith's estate, and won.

Once Viv had money in the bank again, she found the spending obsession was still with her – 'it's like being an alcoholic,' she claimed. Though she knew the capital she had could not last for more than five years, she couldn't resist buying a new car every now and then. She admitted she got depressed because, now, she knew what good living was like. She never wanted to go back to the sweet factory.

Since Keith died, Viv has had four more husbands, been widowed three times and divorced once. Now she lives in a modest terraced house in Victoria Street, Castleford, and has become a Jehovah's Witness. And the money? 'I don't think I'd want to win it again,' she admits.

Norah Docker

At the 1951 Motor Show in London the brightest, costliest exhibit was a huge 36-horsepower Daimler that not only glistened like gold but was actually *covered* in gold. It was a present from Daimler's chief, Sir Bernard Docker, to his wife, Norah. Twenty ounces of 18-carat gold plate covered the headlights, door handles, radiator, window edges, wheel discs and even the bumpers. Seven thousand gold stars were painted on the bodywork. It was fitted with a golden cocktail set and upholstered in yellow silk brocade. The coachwork was superb, and the workmanship splendid. But, people asked in whispers, wasn't it just a shade *vulgar*? 'Nonsense,' dismissed Lady Docker. 'Remember we travel abroad a great deal and this will show people what England can do.'

If anyone was going to enjoy riding around in a gold-plated Daimler it would have to be Norah Docker. Her impulsive, extravagant behaviour made her the darling of the gossip columns for more than a decade. She managed to get herself and Sir Bernard banned from Monaco and the Côte d'Azure, banned from the royal enclosure at Ascot, banned even from their local public house when they went to live in Jersey.

Flaunting her wealth, creating scenes, making life difficult for the patient, good-natured husband who adored her, was all par for the course as far as Lady Docker was concerned; but, in the end, it brought about Sir Bernard's business downfall and the loss of his position as Chairman and Managing Director of BSA.

Despite everything, Norah had an engaging personality and was generous to a fault. It was just that she genuinely enjoyed kicking up a bit of a rumpus. She was usually forgiven, for she was a pretty woman with fair curly hair, wide hazel eyes and a peachy complexion. Her good looks enabled her to find no less than three rich husbands.

Life had not always been gold-plated for her. She was born Norah Turner in a flat above a butcher's shop in Derby. Her father was a car salesman who got into difficulties and committed suicide. For a time, her mother ran a public house. Norah's first job was as a trainee milliner at Bobby's Store in Southport, but she already had grand ideas even then. Nothing but the best, she decided, would do for her. The problem was, how to get it.

Sir Bernard and Lady Docker and (inset) the infamous gold Daimler.

85

Tossing aside her career in hats she went to London, intending to be an actress, but ending up as a dancing partner at the Café de Paris. Men found her very attractive, but she was only interested in the rich ones. In her autobiography she explained her strategy: 'When other girls would be satisfied with fur, I always demanded mink; when other girls would be satisfied with a zircon, I would insist on a diamond. I always asked for champagne, and it had to be pink because I loved the colour.'

At the Café de Paris she met her first husband, Clement Callingham, Chairman of Henekey's, the wine and spirit merchants, and a married man. They lived together before marriage and Callingham's wife cited her in a divorce action as co-respondent. When their son, Lance, was born in 1939 they celebrated the event with 500 bottles of champagne.

Clement Callingham died in 1945 and just over a year later, when she was forty, she married Sir William Collins, head of Cerebos Salt and Fortnum and Mason. Their union began inauspiciously with a row at Caxton Hall register office. He said something about her dress and she threw back at him the pearls he had given her as a wedding present. Things calmed down, but the marriage was never peaceful. After one tiff he cut her out of his will, leaving her a paltry £500. An illness softened his attitude and he restored her to favour. He died, however, when they had only been married for two years.

Now a rich widow with a fast growing son, she decided she must find another husband quickly – 'Women can't bring up boys properly.' At the same time she was terrified of fortune hunters. She decided if she could track down a man richer than herself, she could be sure of being married for love, not money. So she went husband hunting and one night saw Sir Bernard Docker dancing at Ciro's. She knew immediately he was the man for her and admitted, 'I began to haunt him like the family ghost. Wherever he was, I turned up.' At last, he took her out to lunch. Going out together became a habit, but not a word of love was exchanged and she began to feel he was not interested. Just when she was about to give up, he was jolted into action.

Norah had gone off alone to Sweden on holiday. On the return journey her plane had to make a forced landing miles from anywhere. The passengers were stranded for 48 hours. No sooner was she back in London than Sir Bernard was on the phone: 'Thank God you're safe,' he shouted. 'Will you marry me?'

So, at forty-three, she became the wife of the most distinguished of all her husbands. Sir Bernard Docker was not only Chairman of BSA but a senior director of the Midland Bank. He had interests in many other companies besides. She was particularly impressed by the fact that he owned one of the biggest and most luxurious yachts in the world, the 863-ton *Shemara*, and also had a fine country house at Stockbridge in Hampshire. He had been married once before, to actress Jeanne Stuart.

The Dockers flew the family flag from the masthead at Stockbridge and villagers referred to them jokingly as 'the King and Queen'. But a great deal of their leisure time was spent aboard the *Shemara*. It was often anchored in the harbour at Monaco while they played the tables in the casino at Monte Carlo.

Lady Docker had her first blazing row with the principality's officials in 1951. They had been invited to attend the annual Red Cross gala at the casino. Half-way through Norah began to protest in a loud voice that the cabaret was 'awful' and 'nothing better than a fashion parade'. There was a scuffle after the Casino Sporting Club President, Prince Jean-Louis Faucigny-Lucinge, told Sir Bernard: 'Take your wife away.' Lady Docker slapped a Casino official across the face and exploded, 'How dare you! We will never come in here again!'

Despite this, the Dockers were invited to the wedding of Prince Rainier of Monaco and Grace Kelly in 1953 but, again, there was a row when they were refused admission to the casino later that night, and Lady Docker caused yet another scene.

Five years later came the worst row of all. The Dockers had been invited to the christening of Prince Rainier's son and heir, Prince Albert. As it was Lance's 19th birthday Norah took him along as well, only to be told that he could not attend the reception. This infuriated Her Ladyship, who stomped off to have lunch at the Hôtel de Paris. On the table was a small flag in the Monaco colours. She snatched it up, tore it to bits and threw it on the floor. The action was taken very seriously. She was thereafter banned from the principality and, because of a certain treaty, that meant also from the Côte d'Azure. The Dockers' christening gifts were delivered back to their hotel in Cannes. Lady Docker said she didn't care; she'd always preferred Capri anyway.

The Dockers were regular attenders at Ascot and were usually welcomed in the royal enclosure. They were shocked, therefore, in 1953, to be told that the Duke of Norfolk was not going to issue them with the usual badge. Someone, digging up the past, had suddenly realized that Norah had been the co-respondent in her first husband's divorce case. Lady D. decided to put a brave face on it. She went badgeless to Ascot in her new sapphire mink with a saphhire silk dress and a hat made entirely of lacquered shells to match. Just as she had intended, she was the centre of attention. 'This year above all I was determined to get my picture in the papers,' she told everyone. She and Sir Bernard lunched at the Marlborough Club tent, then walked around with the other cash customers in the paddock. One or two loyalists came over from the enclosure to join them. At the end of the day Norah said she had never enjoyed Ascot so much before.

Her every move, her every whim was reported. She twice became the world's women's marbles champion. She was elected Palm Beach Princess. She still created scenes. One night she walked out of the Café de Paris because Labour MP Bessie Braddock, famous for her ample and splendid girth, turned up in day clothes instead of evening glamour.

Just as people were getting tired of her tantrums she would do something that would restore her popularity. She and Sir Bernard went to visit miners down the pit at the Walter Haigh Colliery near Leeds. As a 'thank you' for the warm Yorkshire hospitality they had received, the Dockers invited the miners to join them for a day's outing on board the *Shemara*. Norah entertained them regally with roast chicken and champagne, and strawberries and cream. To loud cheers, she performed a lively version of the sailors' hornpipe.

Less well received was the news that leaked out in 1954. They had to issue a statement through their solicitors explaining their presence at a bizarre and much publicized party given in a Soho restaurant by Mr Billy Hill, a self-styled boss of London's underworld. The party had been arranged to celebrate the publication of Hill's autobiography. Among the guests were several CID officers and some well-known characters from London's underworld, including 'Johnny Up the Spout', 'Three Pints Rapid' and 'The Monkey'.

Lady Docker and Sir Bernard were seen sipping champagne and obviously enjoying themselves. At the end of the evening Billy Hill kissed her on the cheek as she thanked him for a most enjoyable time. Next day came their statement saying they had no idea Billy Hill was going to be their host; indeed, they had never heard of him; they had been misled into going to a party they would otherwise not have considered attending.

Gaffes such as this, and all the other publicity he had received since marrying the irrepressible Norah, had not helped Sir Bernard in his business life. Suddenly, in 1953, he resigned his directorship of the Midland Bank after a dispute with the board.

Three years later came trouble with BSA. The directors had not been very pleased about the publicity surrounding the gold Daimler Sir Bernard had built for his wife. They thought their product too dignified for such treatment. Nor did they appreciate the way in which Lady Docker made a habit of inspecting BSA factories and attending executive parties to which other wives were not invited.

When she heard of the boardroom move to depose Sir Bernard, Norah believed it was because they were jealous of her husband and, without his knowledge or consent, hired private detectives to investigate the activities of the other directors. It was to no avail. A resolution to sack him was carried by six votes to three at a board meeting in June 1956.

Norah sent a letter to 17 000 shareholders, pointing out to them the huge increase in BSA profits since he took over. Sir Bernard himself made an appeal on television. But, at an extraordinary meeting of the shareholders, the board's decision was upheld.

Norah was infuriated by one issue that had been given particular prominence in the affair. They had criticised her for presenting a bill for £7910 for dresses worn at the Paris motor show to publicize the golden Daimler. She protested that she had gained enormous publicity for the company. 'In the end,' she said, ruefully, 'the only battle I lost was that against jealousy!'

The Dockers continued to enjoy country life in Hampshire and cruised around the world in the *Shemara*, but in 1959, the year after the row over the Monaco flag incident, something equally unpleasant happened. Lady Docker lost more than £100 000 worth of jewels.

Norah was in the habit of taking her valuables with her when she travelled. On 10 March 1959 they were staying at a hotel in Southampton. Their Rolls Royce was left in the car park. The jewellery, including two sapphire and diamond necklaces, a sapphire bracelet, emerald bracelets and ear-rings and a solitaire diamond given to her by her second husband, Sir William Collins, was hidden in briefcases and covered with rugs. There were no visible signs that the locks had been tampered with. Lady Docker was in a state of near collapse. 'They've taken everything I've got,' she wailed.

Sir Bernard eventually resigned from most of his business interests, sold the *Shemara* and took his wife to live in the tax haven of Jersey. Norah was still sparking on all cylinders, however, and one day became involved in an argument with a popular singer of the day called Yana, whose husband kept a restaurant. Afterwards, she received a letter saying she was no longer welcome to dine there. The Dockers left for Palma, Majorca, with Norah calling the inhabitants of Jersey 'the most frightfully boring, dreadful people that have ever been born.'

In 1974, she was involved in a libel case after a Sunday newspaper suggested she had been thrown out of a Jersey hotel for using 'naughty words'. She was awarded damages of ½p and ordered to pay her own costs.

After that, the sparkle seemed to leave Lady Docker. The champagne days were over and there was not the same amount of money to splash around. They had a pleasant life on Majorca for a while, but then Sir

Norah was forced to stay on in Majorca, because of the tax situation.

At seventy-one, she was living alone in her rented apartment on Majorca while eighty-one-year-old Sir Bernard gradually became bedridden and blind in a Bournemouth nursing home. She phoned him four times a week and visited him twice a year, at Christmas and in the summer. Their reunions were always affectionate and moving.

'When I telephone Sir Bernard I always put on my bright chat voice,' she told *Woman* magazine in an interview. 'But afterwards, when I put down the receiver, the truth hits me and I sit here and cry.'

Looking back over her remarkable life, Lady Docker admitted sadly, 'I never dreamed it would end like this. I thought the halcyon days would go on for ever. I thought Bernard was indestructible. I thought I was, too.'

Sir Bernard Docker died in May 1978. Five and a half years later, in December 1983, Lady Docker joined him. She was buried beside him in the tiny village churchyard at Stubbings, near Maidenhead in Berkshire. Only 29 people turned up for the funeral, including her son, Lance Callingham, and his family. But none of the 'friends' who had helped her drink the champagne in the 'halcyon days' were there. It was a quiet, tasteful end for such a glittering lady. As she said at the end of her autobiography: 'The party is over. On to the next one.'

Chapter Four

ALL THAT GLITTERS . . .

The wicked men and women, whose lust for riches led them to a life of extortion, cruelty . . . and even murder.

'If you would know what the Lord God thinks of money, you have only to look at those to whom he gives it.'

Dorothy Parker (1958)

'Baby Doc' Duvalier

The wedding of Jean-Claude 'Baby Doc' Duvalier, President For Life of Haiti, in June 1980, was an occasion of such lavish splendour that it was entered in the *Guinness Book of Records*. It was said to have cost three million dollars. Duvalier's bride, Michèle, a glamorous *mulatto* with huge dark eyes, a perfect figure and long painted fingernails, wore a white Givenchy gown and a stunning head-dress like a sunburst of white silk lilies-of-the-valley.

Down in the slums of Haiti's capital city, Port au Prince, television sets had been provided at street corners so that the Haitian people could enjoy the ceremony. Free soup and rum were handed out in the surrounding towns and villages.

If the Haitians' enthusiasm was somewhat muted, it was understandable. They were the inhabitants of the poorest, saddest place on earth, a place Graham Greene had described in *The Comedians* as 'a nightmare'. Of the six million people living there 90 per cent had barely enough to subsist on. While the Duvaliers entertained their guests with the finest imported delicacies, the people went hungry. Many had a hot meal only once a week; the rest of the time they filled their stomachs with what they could lay their hands on, sometimes just fetid water and biscuits made of sand.

The wedding was only a hint of what lay beneath the surface. During the 15 years he was in power, Duvalier and his family misappropriated $120 million of Haitian money. Investigators found it stacked away in private bank accounts all over the world. They also found that Jean-Claude had bought a two-and-a-half-million-dollar apartment in Manhattan, a French château, three Paris apartments, two apartments in New York and Florida, a yacht, a power boat and 100 000-dollar Ferrari.

Lust for money became as bad as a voodoo curse for the baby-faced dictator until he was deposed and sent packing with his greedy womenfolk. With a new Haitian government suing him for the return of all he had stolen, he had to seek asylum in any country that would take him.

Yet when, at the age of nineteen, Jean-Claude Duvalier succeeded his father, the hated 'Papa Doc', there was a certain hope in the air. Since 'Papa Doc' had taken control of Haiti in 1957, the Caribbean island had been under a pall of fear. A former country doctor, he had gained power by

President Jean-Claude Duvalier, flanked by his Ton Ton Macoutes.

preaching black pride and calling upon the gods of voodoo. He was a megalomaniac who ruled with the aid of the dreaded Ton Ton Macoutes. These young thugs in their dark glasses and soft slouch hats were despatched to deal with anyone who uttered a word against his tyranny. 'Papa Doc' called himself Baron Samedi, Lord of Death, and had his opponents' heads brought to him to gloat over. When he died, people whispered with relief, 'Thank God.'

His son Jean-Claude had been brought up in an appalling atmosphere of cruelty and corruption. But he was of a different kind to his father; he was no killer. At first it seemed as though he was setting out to improve things. It looked as though there would be welcome changes. The activities of the Ton Ton Macoutes were curtailed; media censorship was eased; political prisoners were released and there were talk of reforms.

But it turned out the baby faced, overweight young man was not of the stuff to withstand the temptations laid before him. Two women had strong influence over the immature dictator. One was his ruthless mother, 'Mama Doc' Simone Duvalier, who was desperate to keep what power she still had; the other was his wife, Michèle.

Jean-Claude had known Michèle ever since they were at school together. She belonged to one of the fringe upper-class Haitian families and for a time she had worked abroad gaining sophistication and a taste for expensive jewellery and clothes. On returning from America she had only one ambition: to get 'Baby Doc' for a husband. Her sexual prowess, combined with visits to the voodoo priests, were rumoured to have made her job easy. From the moment she became First Lady, Michèle set out to plunder government funds with the aid of her besotted husband. She spent millions of dollars in New York and Paris, buying vast crystal chandeliers and antiques for the presidential palace. (She specialized in Egyptian artefacts.) Givenchy gowns, fur coats and Boucheron jewels were stuffed into vast trunks to be taken back to Haiti.

They lived in an immense two-storey private apartment in the glistening white National Palace on the hill above Port au Prince. The ornate reception rooms were hung with Michèle's Louis XIV crystal chandeliers. The master bedroom contained a floor-to-ceiling safe for her jewellery. There was a private medical suite, a beauty salon and a master bathroom fitted with a jacuzzi and fixtures of lapis lazuli and gold. Meals were prepared in ja high-tech kitchen with computerized equipment.

Soon it became apparent that both Jean-Claude and Michèle were living a delusion. While he congratulated himself on the improvements he was making for his country, she had modelled herself on Eva Perón, wife of the former dictator of Argentina – 'because she was liberal minded and socially aware'. One of her favourite projects was Bon Repos, a small obstetrics clinic on the outskirts of Port au Prince. To raise money for it, she staged a charity ball, the first gala of its kind in Haiti. Tickets cost $500 each – nearly twice the average income on the island – and it was a sell-out. The 'elite' of Haiti were there with their wives in couture gowns and diamonds; guests flew in from other Caribbean islands and Michèle's jeweller, Alain Boucheron, sat beside her at dinner. Once again public television sets were installed, this time throughout the island, so that Haitians could see what their First Lady was doing for them. Immediately after the ball there were riots in the streets of the poorest towns and villages. Michèle could not understand. The money raised was going straight into her Foundation and would be used to improve the clinic. But revolution was in the air. The hungry and impoverished Haitians were angered by the fleeting television images of junketing at the National Palace. Later, an official was to confirm that 'no cheques; not one' were ever placed in the Bon Repos account by the First Lady.

In Haiti's hospitals the poor were often not treated unless they could provide their own bandages and medicines. Yet, according to Duvalier's phoney cheques, hundreds of thousands of dollars went to the island's hospitals and towards social work.

Jean-Claude and his closest associates continued to siphon off millions of dollars a year from public funds. The Duvaliers themselves had blank cheque books by means of which they could draw from any government account, then simply wire the money out of the country.

At first, 'Baby Doc' did not pay a great deal of attention to the reported unrest. He declared: 'I am as strong and firm as a monkey's tail.' His mother 'Mama Doc' thought otherwise. The tough old lady always said that her son was not strong enough to rule, not like his father, who got rid of opponents by killing them and who always kept a Bible and a loaded pistol on his desk.

As revolution gathered pace Michèle, still modelling herself on Eva Perón, drove through the slums throwing coins into the crowd. But she spoiled her act immediately afterwards by taking a dozen friends to Paris for a mammoth shopping spree, a jaunt that cost the government treasury just under $2 million.

By the beginning of 1986, as the economy worsened and commodity goods were running out, there was a great deal of student unrest, followed by riots in the streets. The poor joined in, heartened by the fact that they had found a new ally in Pope John Paul II, who was crusading through the world opening his arms to the wretched.

Determined not to lose face, the Duvaliers drove through the streets of

Port au Prince in their limousine telling reporters on their return that 'the people were really happy to see us.' But when the riots grew worse and it looked as though Haiti would go up in flames, 'Baby Doc' knew the end was drawing near.

Various governments had been watching the events in the Caribbean with concern. Now the US State Department and the French government combined to persuade Duvalier to quit the island while he still had time. He agreed to go, but first insisted on throwing a champagne party at the palace for his friends. On 7 February 1986 at 3.30 in the morning Jean-Claude and Michèle walked across the tarmac at the airport, named after 'Papa Doc', with a suitcase each. They were taken off the island in a US aircraft and landed in the south of France. The First Lady complained she had had to leave everything behind, but in fact, her father, who controlled Air Haiti, had sent on ahead a planeload of jewels, paintings and furs.

From now on they were in exile, the object of curiosity, but shunned by those who knew what their name signified. The French gave them sanctuary until another country would offer to take them. They had been warned not to set foot on American soil. As soon as it was known they had been deposed, financiers and bankers throughout the world moved swiftly to freeze their assets. But investigators feared they might not have been quick enough; 'Baby Doc' still seemed to be able to raise money.

Most of the Duvalier family followed the President and his First Lady into exile, including their two children and 'Mama Doc', who had never got on with Michèle. Finding a suitable house where they could all live temporarily until the French government decided where to send them, was not easy. Most people had heard of 'Baby Doc' and did not want to do business with him. Eventually they rented a rambling but undistinguished house from Mohamed Kashoggi, son of Adnan Kashoggi, the Saudi arms merchant. It was situated just off the autoroute, next to a lettuce farm in the hill town of Mougins, just above Cannes.

Marooned behind a high wall, ignored by the locals and forced to use a false name whenever they went out, life has not been easy for the Duvaliers in exile. They have all the mod cons and a swimming pool, but 'Baby Doc' is bored much of the time and his wife smokes too many menthol cigarettes in order to steady her nerves. The days are empty but Jean-Claude has one thought that should occupy all his waking hours: the new government in Haiti has promised to sue for the return of every single dollar he owes them.

George Hudson

A t the peak of the great railway mania in Victorian England a rough, impetuous Yorkshireman, who had once been a draper's assistant, gained such financial power that they called him 'The Railway King'. His 'realm' included three of the great railway systems of the nineteenth century. By 1848, he had spent £30 million – a vast sum at that time – and envisaged spending millions more.

George Hudson of York was greedy for power, and for a time his assets went up and up. It seemed as though nothing could stop him. His enemies referred to him as 'The Yorkshire Balloon' and he was caricatured in *Punch*; but the unbiased could see that he also had a vision for a future in which railways would play a great part, and that gave him real stature.

The rise and downfall of George Hudson were equally spectacular. Considering that the financial morals of the time were those of a Wild West gambling saloon and the railways were largely built on the profits of commercial corruption, he was unlucky to have been made a scapegoat for economic decline. But having made so many enemies, through his flamboyant behaviour and Yorkshire bluntness, he took the brunt of the blame for what happened.

Hudson always said that the happiest days in his life were when he stood behind a shop counter and when his speculations were confined to silks, satins and laces. But his boundless ambition would never have let him stay there. He had to go on until he became one of the richest men in Britain.

His father was a prosperous farmer at Howsham, a tiny village between York and Malton in the Yorkshire wolds. When George was born, in 1800, it was presumed he would one day follow in his father's footsteps. Farmer Hudson, however, died suddenly and the family had to make new plans to take into account their straightened circumstances. At fifteen, George left home and became apprenticed to a draper, William Bell, in College Street, York. Though boorish in manner, George was hard-working and was eventually offered a permanent job with a small share in the profits. Bell had taken a partner in the business, a man called Nicholson, whose sister came to work in the shop. Hudson married her in 1821. When Bell retired the firm was renamed Nicholson & Hudson.

If it hadn't been for an immense stroke of luck, George Hudson might

A portrait of George Hudson, the 'King of the Railways'.

have spent the rest of his life as a successful draper. In 1827 his great uncle, Matthew Bottrill, died at the age of seventy, leaving him £30 000, his handsome 17th-century house, Monkgate, which, surrounded by a small deer park, stood just outside the city walls. There was also some land including a small farm. Bottrill's other relatives were furious, but they could not prove that Hudson had used undue influence upon the old man, and the will finally went uncontested.

By the age of twenty-seven, the portly young linen draper had become a 'man of consequence' in York. He began calling himself George Hudson Esq., changed from being a Nonconformist to an Anglican, and made himself a leading light among the local Tories. His speeches were said to have been 'crude, blunt and overbearing', but they also showed a distinct authority. By shrewd assessment, he soon learned which men should be accorded deference and which he could treat with the powerful self-confidence which was his true nature.

Quite rapidly, he built up a reputation as an entrepreneur, first by dabbling in importing foreign grain. His most important move, however, was when he turned his attention to banking and in 1833, with several associates, opened the York Union Banking Company which would one day finance the various railway speculations in which Hudson was to become involved.

The first completely steam passenger railway – the Liverpool and Manchester – had been opened in September 1830 in the presence of the Duke of Wellington and Sir Robert Peel. To all forward thinking men it seemed obvious that this was the future, but for three years the City Fathers of York dithered, afraid that their quiet, ancient citadel would be ruined.

At the end of 1833, a Railway Committee was formed in York, and Hudson was nominated treasurer. From the outset he treated the whole scheme more seriously than his colleagues. Railway fever had got into his blood. He took up most of the few hundred shares that were offered for subscription at the first committee meeting and approached famous engineer, Sir John Rennie, to make a preliminary survey of the country between York and Leeds.

Rennie disappointed Hudson, suggesting that, on the grounds of economy, horses should be used on the line instead of locomotives. In that case, the project would be little more than a glorified tramway. He was almost on the point of giving up when, on a visit to Whitby, he was introduced to the great engineer, George Stephenson.

Stephenson, the father of railways, opened Hudson's eyes to a completely new vision of the future. The two men became firm friends. Hudson was now certain that he could build trunk lines that would connect London with the North and a network of railways that would link up all the major industrial centres of England.

The Committee grew from a small private group, to the Provisional Committee of the York and North-Midland Railway Company. As it awaited Parliamentary approval, Hudson began raising capital. By the summer of 1836 the new company held its first meeting. Hudson was elected to the board of directors and later became chairman. The following spring the building of the railway line he had envisaged began.

Once Queen Victoria and Prince Albert had given their approval to the new form of travel there was nothing to hold back the businessmen who were ready to go ahead with expansion. The railway boom was on its way. George Hudson was in his glory. York saw him as its benefactor and made him Lord Mayor.

Never had the old city seen such lavish celebrations as those arranged by the new Lord Mayor and his lady. Feasts, banquets and balls followed one after another, the wine flowed and tables groaned under the weight of fine food. The Mansion House and Guildhall were floodlit with gas illuminations for the great occasions. Hudson's wife, who loved a party, did him credit by bedecking herself in elaborate creations of satin and lace.

However, there were rumbles of discontent; it was taking a great deal longer to open the York and North-Midland Railway than had been hoped. As shares sagged, cynics began to suggest that Hudson's mayoral parties – he was now in his second term of office – were a cover-up for gambling speculations based on the share market fluctuations.

The grand opening was held, at last, on 29 May 1839. It was Hudson's day of triumph. Minster bells were rung, flags hoisted, cannons boomed and a gargantuan breakfast was laid on for distinguished guests. Four hundred passengers packed themselves into the inaugural train, which rattled along the track at a reckless 30-40 miles per hour. At South Milford everyone got out to inspect the line, then returned to York for more feasting and celebrating.

Two immense dinners had been prepared, one at a local inn for 'the small fry' and another at the Guildhall for the high and mighty. Hudson presided at the latter, glowing with achievement and revelling in the adulation. George Stephenson sat at his right hand. The banquet started at 4.30 in the afternoon and did not finish until gone 10 o'clock. Hudson told his guests that he had visions of making York the centre of a massive national network of railways.

Glorying in all this, Hudson paid no heed to the jealousy and bad feeling he was stirring up among some members of the community. The Quakers were deeply suspicious of his handling of the Railway Company's finances, the local Liberals were furious at the way he ignored them and many businessmen thought their city was in danger of being taken over by an overbearing ex-draper.

There was no doubt money and success had gone to Hudson's head. He was somewhat dismayed when he failed to be elected Mayor for the third time. To console him, a testimonial of £700 was raised for purchase of an ornate silver candelabra with a record of the city's gratitude inscribed. But he still had his admirers. When Stephenson joined him for the grand opening of the whole North Midlands line on 30 June 1840, he was cheered to a resounding echo.

No longer Lord Mayor, Hudson turned his whole attention to the expansion of the railways. His fame spread from the north of England to the south, and soon it became clear that if anybody wanted a railway built with speed and efficiency, Hudson was the man to do it. By 1844 he personally controlled about one fifth of all the railways in England.

His personal fortune now considerable, he started buying property all over the place. In just over a year he acquired four large country estates on which he planned to set up his sons as country gentlemen. His own place at Londesborough, near Market Weighton, overlooking the Humber Valley, amounted to 12 000 acres. He planned to build a splendid mansion there. Until it was ready, he made do with Newby Park, purchased from Lord Grey.

In his opinion, London was 'an overrated place', but his wealth, his fame and his election as a Tory MP finally steered him towards the capital. On 21 January 1846, he took his seat in Parliament and installed Mrs Hudson in a mansion on the north side of Knightsbridge, said to be the largest private house in London. Albert House, standing where Albert Gate leads into Hyde Park, cost him £15 000 and he spent another £14 000 decorating and furnishing.

Members of London society eagerly accepted invitations to Albert House, partly out of curiosity, but also in the hope of gaining inside information that would help their own speculations on the railways. Many were snobs, who accepted Hudson's lavish hospitality but thought him 'vulgar'. Mrs Hudson, whose homely figure was always dressed in the latest fashions, was considered monstrously extravagant. She also acquired the reputation of a 'Mrs Malaprop', though her verbal accidents were often offset with shewd Yorkshire wit.

They made friends, however, among the true aristocrats. The Duke of Wellington liked Hudson and enjoyed his visits to Albert House. On one occasion, Hudson was dining with the Duke of Richmond and was heard to remark, as he looked down the table towards his host and the Dukes of

Buckingham and Newcastle: 'Three live dukes! Well, I never before sat down with three live dukes.'

Hudson never pretended to be anything but a self-made man, but his great fault was that he often behaved with rudeness and arrogance towards people whose favour he did not need to court. His burly, blue-coated figure was often the centre of awkward scenes in public and in private. He conducted his affairs with incredible energy. In his opinion, mediocrity was against him.

The first half of 1846 saw his moments of greatest glory, depicted in cartoons in *Punch* and *The Illustrated London News*. On the night of 21 March, he attended a brilliant gathering of Royal Society fellows and members at the Marquis of Northampton's house in Carlton Terrace, in London. It soon became apparent that the hundreds of celebrities present had formed themselves into circles around two men. One was George Hudson, the other the Prince Consort. After a time, a gentleman was seen to pass from one group to the other; the Prince had asked to be introduced to Hudson. The former was said to have laughed out loud at the Yorkshireman's brusque wit, something he seldom did in public.

The following July, Hudson met Queen Victoria for the first time, and she, too, was said to have been very impressed with him. He persuaded her to travel on the Eastern Counties Railway from London to Cambridge with Prince Albert, and seized the occasion for a typical display of flamboyance. A special train was fitted out for the occasion. The royal carriage, white and gold outside, had linings and furniture of figured grey satin. Flowers filled every spare corner. As Victoria looked around her, she exclaimed, 'Really, this is most beautiful! It is *most* gratifying.' To celebrate the Queen's acceptance of rail travel, Hudson went back to York where he spent a whole week throwing banquets and entertaining.

While everyone had once fallen over themselves to meet George Stephenson, now Hudson was everybody's darling. From Chesterfield in Derbyshire, where he was living in retirement, George Stephenson wrote a disillusioned note: 'Hudson has become too great a man for me now. I have made him a rich man, but he will soon care for nobody except if he can get money by them.'

By the end of 1846 the country had gone railway crazy. Investment in the railways had almost become a form of gambling – with people speculating with shares. The public was warned by *The Times*, by certain bankers and even by Hudson himself that if expansion continued at such a rate, there could only be a slump in values. The mania was condemned by Parliament – but two thirds of its members were speculators themselves.

Then fortunes began to slip. There were several elements which combined to form the mid-century depression: the failure of the potato crop in Ireland, a shortfall in the American cotton fields and the repeal of the Corn Laws, leading to large imports of foreign corn. Money became difficult to find, and then, only at high rates. One by one, businesses went bankrupt. The railway companies called desperately on shareholders for capital to use in construction, and were refused money.

At first, Hudson's luck held. Or so it seemed. In fact, he had kept going an artificial demand for railways stock by paying dividends out of his capital. He had always been 'unorthodox' in his business methods. If colleagues dared to question his methods he would threaten to retire. By the winter of 1847-8, however, it seems he had over-reached himself. At the February meeting of the Yorkshire and North-Midland shareholders he had to admit that dividends might fall. The following year was to ruin him for good.

The York, Newcastle and Berwick line caused the first real trouble. A committee was formed to investigate Hudson's management when it was discovered that he had been diverting money intended for purchase of Great North of England shares to new construction, and that 2800 of the shares that were actually bought had come from Hudson himself, at a grossly inflated price. Other investigations followed. *The Times* commented acidly: 'All things would seem to portend that Hudson's reign is over. The bladder shows symptoms of collapse.'

Hudson's whole business life came under a microscope. What finally cooked his goose was his careless attitude to keeping accounts. Having an incredible facility for mental calculation where vast sums of money were concerned, he tended to scoff at meticulous bookkeeping and accounting. He was a man of action who despised office work. He was even said to have ordered ledgers to be destroyed as so much waste paper, and to have encouraged a careless attitude in all around him. It brought about his final downfall.

A few voices were raised pointing out that shareholders had known perfectly well that their accounts were being 'cooked' for the purpose of raising the value of shares. But Hudson took the blame when the railway bubble burst. He had committed the cardinal sin: failure.

His decline was as spectacular as his rise. One by one, his great estates were sold off. He was called to give an account of himself in Parliament which, in fact, he did remarkably well. He managed to earn some sympathy, and no criminal proceedings were taken against him. But in York, Hudson Street was re-named Railway Street and the statue which had been planned in his honour was forgotten and left to crumble.

For several years, his health declining, Hudson worked to pay off his principal railway creditors. Attempts to recover his fortune, however, went badly wrong and in the autumn of 1855, leaving Mrs Hudson in shabby lodgings off Belgrave Road in London, he went abroad with plans to build a trunk railway in Spain. He ended up in France, trailing from one Channel port to another, living in cheap rooms and often going hungry to bed. His clothes were tattered, his figure wasted. He would wait for the arrival of the ferry from England, hoping to meet an old friend who would buy him a good dinner.

Hudson's one last attempt to recover his reputation in England went badly wrong. In 1865, hearing that people in Whitby, on the coast of Yorkshire, were sympathetic to his plight, he offered himself as Tory candidate. Just before the election, he was arrested for non-payment of debts and thrown into York prison.

Despite everything, he still had friends. His old arrogance had gone, and hardship had made him a nicer man. A group of those who had remained loyal to him took pity and raised a subscription which was used to buy him an annuity of £600. It means he was able to live comfortably, if modestly, with Mrs Hudson in a small house in London, to visit the Carlton Club where, to his delight, he was re-elected to his old position as Chairman of the Smoking Room, and to hold up his head in the streets.

He died on 14th December 1871, aged seventy-one. His body was taken for burial in Yorkshire, and as his funeral procession passed through the streets of York, the bells of the Minster were tolled. He had, after all, been 'The Railway King', and had started the great network that would go on into the future.

Imelda Marcos

Imelda Marcos, wife of the deposed President of the Philippines, has been called everything from 'iron lady' to 'blood sucker'. Out in the streets of New York, where she is expected to make an appearance in court facing fraud charges involving $268 million, Filipino expatriates chorus, 'Meldy, Meldy, you're a witch. You have stolen to get rich.' They are out for her blood.

With her innate sense of theatre, Madame Marcos turns up for the court hearing exquisitely groomed in a long blue dress with a low cut neck, surrounded by solicitous supporters and with two nurses in attendance. Her husband is too ill to attend. She will take the burden on her shoulders. 'I have lost everything,' she cries. 'How can they do this to me!'

Back home in Malacanang Palace, where once she lived like a queen, guards raiding the Marcos's private quarters find some of the belongings she has left behind. There are 3000 pairs of shoes, 35 racks of furs, 500 black brassieres, 200 St Michael girdles, 1500 handbags, perfume by the vat and hundreds of bars of expensive French soap.

Fleeing from the Philippines she simply didn't have time to pack the usual 400 pieces of luggage that would normally accompany her abroad. She had sent some on ahead, of course, but on the plane to Hawaii she carried only one piece of hand luggage into which she had managed to cram a great deal of money, a gold crown studded with diamonds, three tiaras, a million-pound emerald brooch, 60 pearl necklaces, 65 gold watches and 35 jewel-studded rings.

Imelda and her ailing seventy-one-year-old husband Ferdinand started their exile in Hawaii humbly enough in a three-bedroomed house in which every inch of available space was occupied by faithful retainers, and filled with cardboard boxes and suitcases. Before long, they had been moved into a luxurious white-walled retreat overlooking Honolulu.

Called to appear before a New York court to have her fingerprints taken and to be charged with swindling on a gigantic scale, the ex-First Lady travelled by private jet with an entourage consisting of secretaries, two nurses, a publicist, a hairdresser, a priest, maids and lawyers.

In New York she occupies a richly carpeted suite at the Waldorf Astoria hotel, a suite with a formal dining-room, five marble bath tubs and a

105

Mrs Marcos has always considered herself a paragon of beauty.

reception room banked with what must be thousands of dollars-worth of flowers, most of them rare and exotic.

But all is not as it seems. Madame Marcos still insists that she has lost everything; she and Ferdinand cannot get their hands on a single peso. It has been like that for two years. Their assets are completely frozen.

The simple fact is, explains a lawyer, that the Marcos's are living on borrowed funds and the love of well-wishers. The villa in Hawaii came about through an admirer, Doris Duke. The seventy-five-year-old tobacco heiress lent Imelda her plane for the journey to New York, and the bill for the Waldorf Astoria, in the region of £1200 a night, is also being picked up by friends. But now, there are angry people outside the hotel, shouting, 'Meldy, Meldy . . . ,' and for once, Imelda dare not go shopping as she used to, when it was fun to pop into Gucci on Fifth Avenue for 50 pairs of shoes at a time.

According to her biographer, Carmen Bavarro, Imelda's father was a once prosperous copra king who went bankrupt. Her mother, Remedios, had to make some sort of home for them in a garage. For years, Imelda dressed in ragged clothes and often went hungry. She grew into a beauty, however, and realized her looks could raise her from the poverty trap. Having won a beauty contest, partly by buttering up a local politician, she began to assess her chances in the political field. Her major coup was to marry Congressman Ferdinand Marcos.

Imelda came into her own just over 20 years ago, when her husband became President. Her looks, her poise, her clothes were all admired. No one realized that the Marcos's were embarking on a reign that was just an excuse for amassing a private fortune.

Ferdinand Marcos earned the equivalent of £5000 a year, but he was already a wealthy man when he took over in the Philippines. His job conferred the ultimate benefit: immunity from prosecution. It also gave him the opportunity to establish great monopolies, to set up new enterprises conveniently controlled by relatives or associates and to hand out lucrative import licences. There were also, allegedly, huge hand-outs from grateful overseas firms who benefited from nuclear power and military contracts.

Imelda proved to be much more than a beauty queen. As First Lady she obviously enjoyed power and showed glimpses of a toughness that earned her the name 'iron butterfly'. She headed no fewer than 30 profitable government corporations and was a major contractor to the state. Having gained such power, she made sure her family benefited. Two of her brothers were given key jobs, one of them running the privately owned Manila Electric Company, the other being put in charge of the government-controlled gambling industry.

Her legendary extravagance abroad was apparently funded through the Philippine National Bank. Records recovered in the Philippines showed the bank was instructed to pay $26 000 for flowers ordered for her hotel suite, $800 000 for jewellery she had bought in New York in 1982 and $2 million as an advance for a trip abroad.

No wonder red carpets were laid out when she appeared. During one 90-day shopping binge in 1983, Imelda spent a staggering $6½-million in New York and Europe. She has a very fine appreciation of her own beauty and does not care how much she spends trying to preserve and enhance it. Her dressing-rooms at the gloomy Malacanang Palace contained enough furs, jewels, perfumes and cosmetics to stock a department store. Her collection of shoes was unique. One pair, meant for disco dancing, had dazzling lights in the high heels that ran off a little battery.

One of Imelda's favourite artists is Francis Bacon, whose often grotesque paintings depict the neurosis of modern man. She said she particularly appreciated him 'because the ugliness of his work makes you realize how beautiful you and your life are.' One thing she cannot forgive the new President of the Philippines, Mrs Cory Aquino, widow of one of Marcos's murdered opponents, is that 'she doesn't make up, doesn't do her nails'.

When the Marcos's first arrived at their cramped little house in Hawaii, the ex-President would complain about the unfaithfulness of their so-called friends. But Imelda, a devout Catholic, found some comfort. She firmly believed that both she and Ferdinand were divine beings: 'Only because of that have we been able to cope with all the ugliness that has happened to us.'

Chapter Five

TOO MUCH FAME, TOO MUCH MONEY

Pop-stars, movie heart-throbs and film starlets . . . whose dazzling rise to fame and fortune only led them into a world of heartache and despair.

'A celebrity is a person who works hard all his life to become known, then wears dark glasses to avoid being recognized.'

Fred Allen (1954)

Elvis Presley

To the millions who called him 'The King', the death of Elvis Presley in August 1977 came as a mammoth shock, the vibrations of which can still be felt today. At forty-two he was still the great idol of rock'n'roll, a legend of the pop world who had made millions from his talent.

It was only when the announcement was made – that Elvis had been found unconscious on the bathroom floor at his mansion in Memphis and had died on his way to hospital – that his admirers world-wide faced the appalling fact that they had actually been watching the slow death of the old Elvis they worshipped for some time. Gone was the snake-hipped, raunchy young man with insolent eyes and curled lip, who could whip up emotions that caused riots. In his place, they had been seeing a parody of the original: an obese figure corsetted into white satin cowboy suits, his face puffed, his eyes blurred with drugs.

Many believed that Elvis had been killed by an overdose of fame, by sycophantic friends who would not make him face the truth, by isolation amidst the rich trappings that his career had brought him. It was the sort of tragedy that could only have happened in the era of pop culture, when a bashful young truck driver from Memphis could, in 21 years, become a 'King' in his own right.

During the last part of his life Elvis hated to leave Graceland, the opulent, 20-roomed mansion in Memphis, where he was watched over by a group of dubious friends and bodyguards. He had other homes in Bel Air, Hollywood, Palm Springs, California, and a 163-acre ranch in Mississippi. He also had a jet aircraft converted to his own special needs, a fleet of 37 cars and dozens of trucks. But in the end, he preferred to sit watching TV while he stuffed himself with pizzas, cheeseburgers, bacon sandwiches and cream cakes. It was hard to believe that this was the same Elvis, America's favourite legend – the small-town boy who loved his mother, served his country, made good and never forgot his roots. Some say that it was the death of his mother, Gladys Presley, that started the rot. At the beginning it was she who had, unwittingly, started him on the road to fame.

Elvis was born in a two-roomed shack in Tupelo, Mississippi, on 8 January 1935, the only surviving twin son of share cropper Vernon Presley

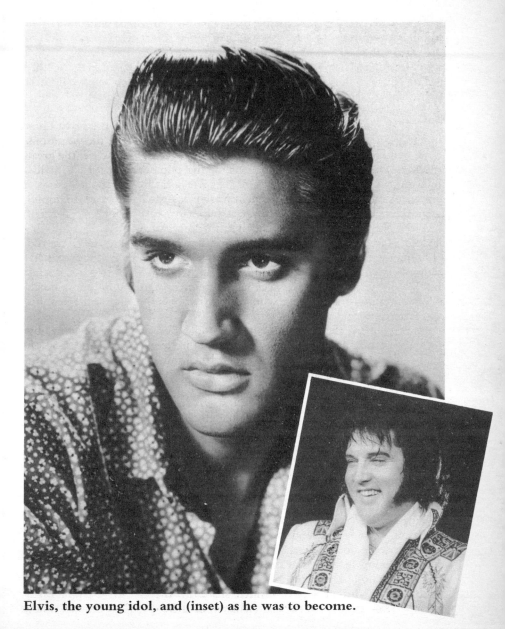

Elvis, the young idol, and (inset) as he was to become.

and his wife, Gladys. When the boy was thirteen, his family moved to Memphis where his impoverished father hoped to get work. Elvis did not distinguish himself at high school, but he loved to sing and showed a distinct talent for music. To encourage him, Gladys scraped enough money together to buy her shy, gangling son a 12-dollar guitar, with which he gave his first performances, either at home or at the First Assembly of God Church which he attended with his parents.

When he was eighteen, Elvis got a job as a truck driver. For the first time ever, he had money in his pocket to buy his mother a birthday present. After some thought, he decided to make her a record. He went to a small studio in Memphis, run by a man called Sam Phillips, and for $4 made a disc recording of a song called *My Happiness*. Phillips listened to the play-back and sat bolt upright in his chair. For years he'd been looking for a 'black sound inside a white boy'; now he'd found it. 'But I never knew he was going to be *that* big. None of us knew he was going to be that big,' he said, years later.

Phillips called Elvis back to the studio, and out of the next few sessions they recorded together came *That's All Right, Mama*, which was a big hit locally. Since Elvis had never had any tuition, and mixed up half a dozen styles in his performance, guitarist Scotty Moore and bass player Bill Black were hired to work with him. For nearly two years the three of them went on tour together, travelling in a clapped-out Cadillac, pooling what money they had to buy hamburgers and cadging lifts when their car broke down. Elvis, shy and diffident off stage, turned into a different species in performance. His confidence increased with every concert. There was a raw energy about his voice, a low pulse that hit the gut

One night in Memphis he started to sway, hips swivelling, pelvis shaking. Before he had finished, he had the audience hanging from the rafters.

Elvis Presley's impact was still confined to the southern states of America when he was introduced to Colonel Tom Parker at the end of 1955. Parker, shrewd entrepreneur that he was, booked Elvis for his first big tour – Hank Snow's All Star Jamboree. Then he stood back and watched. From the moment Elvis came on stage, the show lit up. Girls in the audience shrieked, cried and moaned as rock'n'roll was delivered in a way they'd never heard before. Before the year was out, Parker had become Presley's manager. 'You stay talented and sexy,' he is reported as saying, 'and I'll make amazing deals that will make us both as rich as rajas.' Within a few months Colonel Parker had kept his word.

At the time the Colonel first took Elvis in hand, the singer was still a very rough diamond. His clothes were wild and flashy, his black hair was plastered back in a 'DA', his skin was sallow from sleepless nights. Parker changed all that. The Elvis he presented to the world was a handsome young man, immaculately dressed with a lick of black hair falling carelessly over a pair of sleepy, sexy eyes. On stage he was a threat to the virtue of everybody's daughter; off stage he was diffident, polite, a boy from Memphis who was devoted to his mother.

Once Parker had got him on the Ed Sullivan TV show, watched by half the population of America, he then negotiated one of the most controversial contracts ever known in the recording industry. By skilful handling, Elvis was released from his contract with the man who had discovered him, Sam Phillips, and signed up with the giant RCA-Victor record label. The sum involved was said to be the highest ever paid for a contract release in the field of music. In the winter of 1956 Elvis made *Heartbreak Hotel*, the record generally considered to have sent him into orbit.

Controversy raged around him from the start. Idolized by the young, who saw him as part of their teenage rebellion, he was described as lewd, suggestive and disgusting by disapproving parents. The rotating pelvis, which drove his fans wild, was attacked by churchmen, TV critics, columnist Hedda Hopper and just about everybody else you could think of. He was accused of 'sexually setting young women on fire', and evangelist Billy Graham said: 'From what I've heard, I'm not so sure I want my children to see him.' The storm only died down when Presley was promoted on TV as a decent, well-mannered, Bible-reading boy.

In the same year as *Heartbreak Hotel* was released, Elvis made his first film, *Love Me Tender*, to be followed by at least 30 more, many of which squandered his unique talent and aimed for middle-of-the-road mass audiences. Money was pouring in from all sides as the Colonel manipulated Elvis and his career. Perhaps for the first time, the young truck driver from Memphis began to realize that superstardom would cost him. He was rushed from concert to concert in luxury high speed cars, stopped from giving Press interviews, locked behind hotel doors and surrounded by a watchful band of record executives and moneymen.

It was the US Draft that gave Elvis a brief respite from Colonel Parker's regime. In March 1958 he was called up for the Army and, attended by maximum publicity, had his hair cut to regulation length and donned a uniform. He had never looked more handsome.

The following August, however, his world seemed to collapse when his mother, Gladys, died. She had always been the most important person in his life. With his first money, he had bought her a Cadillac, so that she could ride about in style. He had planned to turn her into the queen of Memphis. He could not come to terms with the fact she was gone.

Still suffering from the emotional blow of his mother's death, Elvis was

113

sent to Germany in 1959. There he met, and began dating, fourteen-year-old Priscilla Beaulieu, daughter of a career air force officer. Though he was the idol of millions, he was desperate to be loved for himself and Priscilla's youth and innocence seemed to guarantee pure love in his eyes. She also had what he recognized as 'class'.

According to most sources, Elvis took full advantage of the women who offered themselves to him. He once bragged that he'd been to bed with 1000 women. But the girl he married had to be different. He wanted to put her on a pedestal, in place of the mother he had lost.

Priscilla was still a schoolgirl when she went to live with Elvis at Graceland. She was his living doll. During the day, she wore convent school uniform. At night, she changed into gold lamé and black velvet. Colonel Parker nearly went mad when he discovered how young she was, but Priscilla states, quite categorically in her autobiography, that Elvis did not make love to her until they married.

Though professing admiration for Priscilla's natural kind of beauty, he started to turn her into his idea of a glamorous woman. Her hair was darkened and piled up into the beehive shape fashionable at the time, her eyes outlined with thick black make-up. They went shopping together and he spent fabulous amounts on clothes that were much too old for her, much too elaborate.

At Christmas 1966, Elvis proposed, and they were married the following April at an early morning ceremony in Las Vegas. He had insisted that the simple white wedding dress she had chosen was fitted with a 6-foot train and that her plain bouffant veil be held in place by a rhinestone crown. 'You look like a fairy queen,' he whispered to his bride at the altar.

Elvis was worried that marriage would spoil his image, but he kept his wife so far in the background that his fans soon forgot her. The birth of their daughter, Lisa Marie, on 1 February 1968, made him more determined than ever to keep his family in a gilded cage. He would buy them anything in the world, and loved them in his own way; but he never gave them anything of himself.

There was no privacy at Graceland. Elvis was always surrounded by aides and managers and hangers on. He would stay up all night listening to records, playing cards, talking over the good times they'd had 'on the road'. It got so bad that he had to take pep pills to keep himself awake and more pills to get a few hours sleep.

Six months of the year he would be away on tour. Tour members' wives were banned, and Priscilla, waiting in her gilded cage in Memphis, knew that there were always girls around to keep him company. Elvis had convinced himself that, as the 'King', he had certain fantasies to fulfil, and they included being the great lover.

By the late 1960s, Elvis had become a compulsive spender. He bought and sold hundreds of Cadillacs and Lincoln Continentals over the years, usually at the rate of two a month. The Convair 880 jet aircraft in which he travelled to concerts was fitted with a double bed and other luxuries that cost almost as much as the plane itself. Because he was short-sighted, he bought himself 300 pairs of expensive prescription sunglasses, and when he took up karate he paid $2000 apiece for the jumpsuits he used for practice.

His father, Vernon, who eventually took over the handling of his finances, 'because my boy was getting through too much', would sometimes gasp when the bills came in. 'Hey man, there's plenty more where that came from,' Elvis would retort with impatience.

There probably was. A conservative estimate of his record earnings alone on 3000 million world sales was $30 million. But, deep down, he had fears about whether it could last, whether he could always be 'King'. More wild spending was the only thing that made him feel invincible – and Elvis certainly knew how to spend.

One summer, feeling guilty about leaving Priscilla alone so much, he bought her a horse. She didn't have anyone to ride with, so he bought his cousin, Patsy Presley, a horse, too, so that they could go riding together. Then he bought himself one. In the end, every member of his entourage had a horse. Next came cowboy outfits for everyone, with genuine Stetson hats and leather boots. Within a month, he had acquired a ranch for the horses and a fleet of trucks and trailers. In the end, Priscilla's horse had set off a million-dollar spending spree.

By Christmas 1971, Presley's marriage was on the rocks. He was devoting himself more and more to performing live, only returning home to give his wife unwanted, lavish presents. When he offered to buy her a new car for Christmas, she sighed that he had only just given her a beautiful chocolate brown Mercedes. She didn't want any more cars; she wanted his love. And since Elvis didn't have time to be a loving husband, she finally turned elsewhere for affection.

Elvis never got over the shock of hearing that Priscilla intended to leave him for another man. Karate expert, Mike Stone, who was a pauper compared to Presley, had become the new man in her life. They planned, she told him, to live together. Elvis cried pathetically to everyone in earshot, 'She has everything money can buy – cars, homes, an expense account. And she knows that all she has to do is ask and I'll get her whatever she wants.' He knew the truth well enough. She had wanted him – his time – and he hadn't got it to give. He was too busy creating a legend.

Elvis was angry with himself for losing the woman he loved. He was angry with Priscilla. He was murderously angry with Mike Stone and threatened to kill him, or find someone who would do the job. Although everyone knew he was simply making threats because of hurt and wounded pride, there was deep unease in the Memphis camp. Elvis had an obsession with guns, and, at times, could explode into frightening tempers.

Luckily, the fuse didn't blow. Instead, Elvis just sank into deep depression. By the day of the divorce in October 1973 he had gained control over himself, greeted his wife affectionately and said goodbye to her with a gentle kiss.

People could not help noticing, however, that Elvis looked terrible. He was much heavier, his face was swollen, his eyes were puffy and he was sweating profusely. From that time on, Elvis's physical condition became a matter of concern to all around him.

Just six days after the divorce he was admitted to the Baptist Memorial Hospital in Memphis, the first of many hospital stays. The news bulletin merely said that Elvis had been ordered to rest, but in fact he was a sick man – with a twisted colon, breathing difficulties and blood clots in his legs.

His family and friends begged him to take a break from his heavy schedule, but, for Elvis, that was impossible. Singing was his life. In 1974 he was on the road for six months and did a total of 70 shows, not counting his regular Las Vegas dates. In 1975, again he was touring for four months, doing a total of 50 shows; and in 1976, his peak year, he was performing somewhere every month for ten months of the year. He would drive himself into the ground on tour, then be forced to spend a period in hospital or at Graceland. 'The people around him felt it was like trying to stop a runaway truck, without knowing how to apply the brakes,' writes Robert Gibson in *Elvis, a King Forever*.

During his last years, his only forays into the real world were during carefully insulated concert tours. He was becoming increasingly isolated from reality. At Graceland he was surrounded by the group of aides, managers and 'yes' men that became known as 'The Memphis Mafia', three members of whom eventually defected and revealed all in a book which made him sound like a drugged manic depressive. His routine on tour was usually the same: private plane to private limousine; into the back entrance of a hotel to a specially cleared elevator, to a penthouse suite. After a while he would be whisked off to the concert through a back exit, on to the stage, back to the hotel, then the airport. Reality never intruded, except when something went wrong with the schedule.

He was finding it impossible to control his weight, which at one point, went up to 17 stone. He was still a handsome man with incredible charisma, but all the junk food he consumed compulsively gave him an unhealthy pallor. From morning till night he used drugs as 'medical aids'. There were drugs to make him go to sleep, drugs to control his weight and drugs to control his physical ailments. The tablets, capsules and injections were getting the better of him. At any time medication was withdrawn, Elvis could become violent. By 1977 he was beginning to worry those around him by displaying signs of unbalance, not to be wondered at considering the life he led. Sometimes he would fire a gun into the walls or furniture to let off steam. Sometimes, he imagined he saw the ghost of his mother haunting Graceland.

There was, however, a new love in his life, twenty-year-old Ginger Alden, and he considered marrying again, even getting to the point of buying her a $30 000 engagement ring.

On 26 June 1977, Elvis played his last concert at Indianapolis. Though heavy and sweating profusely, he was in great voice and gave a brilliant performance. The fans went wild, little knowing that they would never see him on stage again.

Back home in Memphis he succumbed to his usual habit of eating mounds of pizzas, cheeseburgers and huge bacon sandwiches. This time his mood was darker than usual, and not even the 'uppers' worked.

The night of 16 August Elvis could not sleep, and he got up to read. He had had a strenuous game of raquetball, which had exhausted him, and not even his usual knock-out pills had any effect. In the early hours of the morning, he was found in his blue silk pyjamas slumped unconscious on his face on the bathroom floor. An ambulance was rushed to the house and attempts were made to revive him all the way to the Baptist Memorial Hospital. His own personal doctor could be heard pleading, 'Breathe Presley, breathe.' But Elvis died, without regaining consciousness, in the resuscitation unit on the ground floor of the hospital.

Elvis Presley was buried near his mother, after the sort of public wake that attended the death of Rudolph Valentino. Eighty thousand fans jammed the streets outside the Memphis mansion, hoping for a view of the body which had been laid out in state: 30 000 were admitted to the house. Dozens fainted from emotion and the heat. After the funeral at Graceland, a cortège of 16 white cadillacs led a slow procession down Elvis Presley Boulevard to the cemetery. Memphis ran out of flowers, and reinforcements had to be sent from California and Colorado.

Elvis was only forty-two when he died but, as someone said at the time, it was perhaps remarkable that he had survived all the rigours, pressures and absurdities of life as the world's king of rock'n'roll for as long as he did.

Marilyn Monroe in the famous *The Seven Year Itch* 'windy' dress.

Marilyn Monroe

On a sultry, hot day in August 1962 the world was stunned to hear that Marilyn Monroe had apparently taken her own life. That radiant, magical, vulnerable sex goddess, with her spun gold hair and laughing eyes, lay dead in a bleak little bedroom, one hand on the telephone, as though even at the last moment she was calling for help. Was it suicide, or a terrible accident? Or even, as sinister voices began to murmer, murder by the CIA? Improbable theories were tossed to and fro. No one wanted to believe she had gone.

Marilyn Monroe had, in a sense, been calling for help throughout her life, but no one had been able to rescue her. By the time she died, from a massive overdose of drugs, her films had earned an estimated $100 million. But money meant nothing to her, and she remained what she had always been beneath the bright, shimmering exterior – a little girl lost.

Breaking out of a deprived childhood to win international stardom, Marilyn grew up to hate the spun sugar image that made her famous and longed to be taken seriously as an actress. Adjectives like 'gentle', 'vulnerable', 'frail', were used to describe her, but she also had tantalizing physical beauty, and was packaged and sold by Hollywood as the greatest cinematic sex symbol of our time.

There were three husbands and many lovers; her name was even linked with that of President Jack Kennedy, as well as his brother Robert, her deep feelings for the latter leading to humiliation and rejection. But at the end she was alone, with only a housekeeper to claim her body. She could never have suspected that after her death, her fame would be even greater and she would be transformed into an icon, a legend, a tragic heroine.

Right from the beginning, life was an unstable affair for the girl who was christened Norma Jeane Mortensen. Her mother, Gladys Pearl Baker Mortensen, worked as a film cutter and technician at various Hollywood studios. She had been abandoned by her second husband, Norwegian born Edward Mortensen, only months after their wedding and had taken up with a salesman, C. Stanley Gifford. He was totally uninterested when she told him she was pregnant. Norma Jeane never knew her father, and he never acknowledged her when she was born on 1 June 1926.

There was a frightening amount of insanity on her mother's side of the

119

Marilyn's pin-up smiles hid the painful tragedy.

family, and Gladys Mortensen, herself, spent much of her adult life in a series of homes for the mentally sick. Norma Jeane was fostered first in one home, then another. Her foster parents were mostly kind, but, nevertheless, failed to make her feel she 'belonged'. The great betrayal came when she was nine years old. Having run away from her foster parents, she was taken to the Los Angeles Orphanage where she remained for 21 months. She remembered screaming, 'I'm not an orphan!'; but it made no difference. The experience scarred her for life.

Her mother's friend, Grace McKee, was named her guardian and eventually rescued her by taking her to live in her home with her new husband, 'Doc' Goddard. Norma Jeane never felt close to Grace, but at least Grace gave her some sense of security.

The woman who really helped Norma Jeane grow up was her Aunt Ana, a gentle Christian Scientist who, though a sixty-two-year-old spinster, understood the turmoil she had gone through and tried to give her much needed love. It was to her that Norma Jeane recounted the trauma of having been raped at the age of eight by a lodger in one of her foster homes. No one else believed her, but in later years Monroe said that being sexually molested as a child made her feel of little value to anyone.

Next door to the house where Norma Jeane lived with 'Aunt' Grace was the Dougherty family. While she was still at high school, one of the unmarried sons, James Edward, began to interest her. He was good-looking, extrovert and possessed a mischievous sense of humour. The attraction was mutual. Jim, six years older than Norma Jeane, was fully aware of her early ripening attractions. When she was sixteen, he proposed. Marriage seemed to her like a safe haven and she accepted. They were married on 19 June 1942.

Norma Jeane seemed perfectly content with being Jim's wife until 1944, when he enlisted as a PT instructor in the US Merchant Marine and took her to live with him in married quarters. Suddenly, she found herself surrounded by young men who stared and whistled when she walked by. Tight sweaters emphasized her curves, and she soon learned how to swing her hips in a provocative way. When she confessed to Jim her ambition to be a film star, he told her to forget it. He was old-fashioned, unimaginative, good, decent – and he didn't have the remotest idea how to cope with her.

When Jim was sent to Shanghai, Norma Jeane stayed with his family and worked in an aeroplane factory at Burbank. One day, a photographer turned up from the Army's pictorial centre in Hollywood. Seeing Norma Jeane, he went to work with his camera. The pictures he took were printed in hundreds of Army newspapers, including *Yank* and *Stars and Stripes*. She was on her way to a career in modelling.

TOO MUCH FAME, TOO MUCH MONEY

Soon, Norma Jeane was appearing in all the leading magazines, her soft brown colouring changed to platinum blonde for the sake of the cameras. At that time, Twentieth-Century Fox were on the look-out for new faces and casting director Ben Lyon, seeing potential in the young model, asked her to make a screen test.

It was Leon Shamroy, top cameraman at Twentieth-Century Fox, who first photographed her for the screen. He made her brush out her pale gold hair so that it caught the light, and put her into a clinging sequinned dress. All she had to do was light a cigarette and walk across the set. It was enough. When Shamroy first saw the 'frames', he felt a cold chill go over him. There was something about her that hadn't been seen on film since the days of Jean Harlow.

For the first six months with Twentieth-Century Fox, Norma Jeane was groomed and processed through the studio publicity machine. Ben Lyon did not like her name. He suggested 'Marilyn' and left her to find the rest. Her guardian, Grace Goddard, called upon to countersign her contract, suggested her grandmother's name, Monroe. So, from August 1946, Marilyn Monroe it was. Two months later she accepted that her marriage to Jim Dougherty had crumbled away, and she got a divorce in Reno.

Monroe's agent in the early days was a man called Johnny Hyde, to whom she always gave credit for launching her on her career. Hyde fell deeply in love with her but, as he was 30 years older, she could only regard him as a father figure and friend. Urged by fellow starlets to accept his proposal of marriage, they asked her, 'What have you got to lose?' She replied, 'Myself'; added, 'I'm only going to marry for one reason –love.'

She despised the men who tried to buy her with money. Spending her own salary on drama, dancing and singing lessons and buying as many books as she could afford, she struggled to improve herself and kill the 'dumb blonde' image that was threatening to engulf her.

Through Johnny Hyde she made the breakthrough from forgettable B films to major productions. He got her her first decent part in *The Asphalt Jungle*, a realistic crime film directed by John Huston. This was followed by a rôle in the famous Bette Davis saga, *All About Eve*. By 1952, playing Lorelei Lei in *Gentlemen Prefer Blondes*, she had graduated to stardom as the quintessential 'dumb blonde'. But she preferred her role in *How To Marry a Millionaire*, because it allowed her to wear glasses and display her talent as a delicious comedienne.

As a famous star, she had her own luxury bungalow on the film set, with a dressing room, bedroom, wardrobe and bathroom. When shooting had finished for the day, she usually went back alone to her suite at the luxurious and expensive Bel-Air Hotel to read and sip champagne.

One night, a girlfriend phoned to say she had fixed them both up with a date. Marilyn's escort was to be Joe DiMaggio, the great Yankee baseball player, who was a national hero. Marilyn tried to excuse herself: she was tired; she had an early start in the morning. But the friend was insistent. *Nobody*, she said, could offend the great DiMaggio in that way.

They were attracted to each other on sight. DiMaggio, already retired at thirty-seven, was in splendid shape, soft spoken with a touch of grey at the temples. Monroe had never been more vital and alive. She was ready for a serious affair. For two years they were almost inseparable, but whenever DiMaggio talked about marriage she steered away from the subject. Apart from making love, they had few interests in common. He did not like the 'phoneys' of the film world and was not very interested in her career. People noticed that he did not even accompany her to the spectacular première of *How to Marry a Millionaire*. They were very much in love, however, and eventually he swept aside her reservations. They were married in San Francisco on 14 January 1954.

Soon after the wedding, Marilyn went on an army morale-boosting visit to Korea, where American troops were bogged down in the aftermath of a bitter war. Throwing off the thick padded jacket she had been offered as a protection against the bitter cold, she sang to thousands of soldiers, wearing the sort of glamorous, low cut dresses they had seen in her pin-ups. They adored her for it.

On her return she found DiMaggio was not impressed. There was a streak of prudery in him and he did not like his women to wear low cut dresses. Some of her film costumes were so tight, she had to be sewn into them; and they barely covered her breasts. He had thought, with marriage, things would change and she would settle down to a more domestic rôle, putting her career second. Disillusionment set in rapidly. DiMaggio sank back into his comfortable bachelor habits and began spending more time with his baseball cronies.

Marilyn started to film *The Seven Year Itch*, a delightful comedy directed by Billy Wilder. Although she had misgivings about the way she was always cast in dumb blonde parts, this rôle had style and class. DiMaggio, however, disapproved of what she was doing on screen. While the film was being made, a promotional photograph was taken of her standing over a subway grating. As the wind from a train passed beneath, it blew her white pleated dress above her sleek, bare thighs. DiMaggio watched from a distance. As her skirt flew higher and higher he turned away, his jaw set in anger. Later that night, guests at the New York hotel where they were staying heard sounds of quarrelling from their room.

They had been married for ten months and it was all over.

123

After the divorce, Marilyn fled Hollywood to study acting with Lee Strasberg at the famous Actors' Studio in New York, where Marlon Brando had also studied. Strasberg taught her to act 'from the inside out'; to *feel* a scene inside herself before she performed. For the first time, she found herself being accepted as a serious actress.

It was then that Marilyn astonished the film industry by forming her own production company, with the hope of being able to find more demanding roles. As 'Marilyn Monroe Productions', she negotiated a new contract with Twentieth-Century Fox that vastly increased her profit and control. She then chose two films far above the usual level. The first was *Bus Stop*, directed by Joshua Logan, for which she gave a superb performance, and the second was *The Prince and the Showgirl*, with Laurence Olivier as her director and co-star.

If the industry was surprised by Marilyn's sudden business acumen, it was set back even more by the announcement of her next marriage. Quietly and persistently, Arthur Miller, America's foremost playwright and a considerable intellectual, had been wooing the sex goddess. They were deeply in love. She married him in White Plains, New York, on 29 June 1956, then again in a Jewish ceremony ten days later. When she left for England to work with Olivier on *The Prince and the Showgirl*, Miller went with her.

Monroe's reputation for being difficult to work with stems from this time. She had come very much under the influence of Lee Strasberg's wife, Paula, who was now her acting coach. Sometimes, everything on set would stop, while Marilyn rushed over to consult her. Never a good time-keeper she now kept camera crews waiting for hours, while she soaked in a bath or compulsively washed and re-washed her hair.

Both Lee and Paula Strasberg had flown to London with the Millers, Lee to reassure Marilyn as she faced the challenge of appearing with the great Olivier, Paula to coach and hand out tranquillizers and sleeping pills. Miller could not stand the Strasbergs, and trouble was brewing even before they left the plane.

Marilyn was terrified of Olivier, and he did nothing to calm her. Although he claimed he treated her as 'an artist of merit', she found the whole experience of working with him a traumatic one. Filming in Hollywood had not prepared her for her encounter with the aristocracy of British acting. She flew to Paula Strasberg every time she wanted advice, forgot her lines and sometimes failed to appear for two or three days at a time, pleading illness. Olivier was beginning to think she was a troublesome shrew. Towards the end, he was a nervous wreck, and even the staunchly supportive Miller had begun to lose patience.

The first crack in the marriage came when Marilyn read an entry in Miller's black notebook, left open by accident. In it, he had written that he had once thought she was 'some sort of angel'; but now he guessed he was wrong.

On the couple's return to America, they lived an idyllic rural life in Miller's beautiful Colonial farmhouse. They had a deep love for each other and Miller hoped that, with the troubled weeks in England behind them, they could settle down to a happy married life. They were both ecstatic when Marilyn found she was pregnant but, tragically, she lost the baby and was soon back to pills and sessions with the analyst.

Miller, sad for her and sympathetic, said he would write a screenplay which would give her a fulfilling acting rôle. He started writing *The Misfits* – a tough, tormented story about two cowboys who round up wild horses to be killed for dog meat. A tender hearted blonde goes with them for the ride and ends up making her protest against what she sees as the destruction of all free, wild things. Clarke Gable and Montgomery Clift were to be her co-stars.

Even as the screenplay was being written Monroe, on her everlasting search for love where she could get it, had started an affair with Yves Montand, who had been her co-star in *Let's Make Love*. Afterwards, the Frenchman ungallantly protested she had pursued him. Whatever the truth, it signalled the end of her four-year marriage to Arthur Miller.

In his complete and thoughtful biography of Marilyn, Fred Lawrence Guiles says at this time Paula Strasberg was telling columnists: 'She has the fragility of a female, but the constitution of an ox. She is a beautiful humming bird made of iron.' Friends of Marilyn were concerned to see this in print, says Guiles. 'She was barely pinned together emotionally at this time and would collapse altogether within a few weeks.'

The Millers both knew if they separated before the film was made, *The Misfits* would be ruined. Marilyn was in limbo throughout the filming. All the stars, it turned out, were doomed. Clark Gable died of a heart attack not long after it was finished; Montgomery Clift ended his life with an overdose. Marilyn was heavily into narcotics and could probably not have got through without the help of Paula Strasberg and Gable, who treated her firmly but like a loving father.

As *The Misfits* came to an end, so did the Miller marriage. She did not realize how much she had depended on Miller for support until he had gone. Now, both physically and emotionally, she began to go to pieces. Her condition became so disturbed that her analyst persuaded her to enter the Payne Whitney Psychiatric Clinic at New York Hospital under the psuedonym Faye Miller. Once inside she began to panic, and turned to her old love Joe DiMaggio for help. When he became aware of the circumstances, he signed her out and took her to stay with friends. As she had no work in the offing, he invited her to join him at his home in Fort Lauderdale, where they went surf fishing. Though DiMaggio had failed her as a husband, he was a staunch friend.

It was now April, 1961. Marilyn closed down her apartment in New York and returned to Hollywood to be greeted by old friends like Frank Sinatra and Peter Lawford. They drew her into the Rat Pack, a group of all-male friends, which also included Sammy Davies Jnr. and Dean Martin. Marilyn became their mascot.

Peter Lawford's wife, Pat, who was a Kennedy, became one of her closest friends. Through her, Marilyn came into contact with the President, Jack Kennedy, and his brother, Bobby, who was then Attorney General. She began a discreet affair with the President, their trysts planned with the greatest secrecy. She knew that for him she was only one of many, for he was a notorious womanizer. It was Bobby, with his intense compassion for people, who interested her most. She felt deeply for him, and began to have daydreams that one day they would marry. When she faced reality, however, she knew he would never ruin himself politically for her. Only a few weeks before she died, he withdrew from the affair as delicately as he could, and carefully avoided a scandal.

In the Spring of 1962, Marilyn started work on a new film for Twentieth-Century Fox. There was a dreadful irony in its title: *Something's Got to Give*. It was a light-hearted story, but from the first the production was bedevilled by her lateness on set, her inability to learn the script and her problems with the director and actors. When she slipped away to make an appearance at President Kennedy's birthday party, singing *Happy Birthday* in a revealing cobwebby dress that sparkled and clung and made the audience gasp, it was the last straw. On 7 June 1962, the studios fired her for wilful violation of her contract.

She struggled on for two months. Other film offers came, but she couldn't make her mind up about any of them. She had bought herself a Spanish-style house, but it was only half furnished and she wandered disconsolately through the unfinished rooms. Nothing in her life was working. Her career was in jeopardy. There was no man in her life and she had stopped caring how she looked.

Some time during the night of 5/6 August she went into the bathroom and took an overdose of barbiturates from the dozens of bottles in her medicine cabinet. She made a few blurred, indistinct phone-calls. These could have been cries for help, but, by the time anyone came to realize, it was too late. The screen goddess was dead.

Mario Lanza

When Louis B. Mayer of Metro-Goldwyn-Mayer first heard the liquid gold of Mario Lanza's voice, he predicted: 'I think we've found a singing Clark Gable.' Mayer was no lover of grand opera, but he knew a star when he saw one and the young Italian with crinkly dark hair and smouldering dark eyes not only had a thrilling classical tenor voice but undoubted appeal for the opposite sex.

Lanza became an overnight sensation. His films earned money beyond his wildest dreams, his records sold by the million and more than once he was compared with his idol, the great Caruso. Tragically, Lanza could not handle the kind of fame and fortune that came to him. At his zenith, one of the biggest stars in Hollywood, he gradually destroyed himself with self-indulgent extravagance, orgies of eating and drinking and womanizing. Only thirty-eight when he died, the circumstances surrounding his last days remain a mystery. His health was wrecked and, as far as the Press was concerned, he had eaten himself into an early grave. After his death, however, it was suggested he might have been a victim of the Mafia.

In his early youth, Mario Lanza stood out from the other 'macho' Italian boys he ran the streets with because of his love of opera. His real name was Alfredo Arnold Cocozza and he was born into an American-Italian family in South Philadelphia, Pennsylvania, on 31 January 1921. By some strange twist of fate, he was christened by a priest named Caruso. His mother, Maria, was only seventeen, his father Antonio ten years older. Eventually, he would adopt his mother's first name and add her maiden name to become Mario Lanza.

His mother's family had emigrated originally from Abruzzi in Italy and prospered enough to open a fruit-and-vegetable shop in Philadelphia. Mario was brought up in a noisy, happy Italian atmosphere in a house where, besides himself and his parents, there were grandparents, five aunts, two uncles and various cousins. Handsome, sturdy, with a mop of black hair, young Mario looked angelic as an altar boy at the church of St Mary Magdalene de Pazzi, the first Catholic church in south Philadelphia; but he was also full of mischief.

At nine years old, he had a glimpse of the darker side of American-Italian life. His father's brother, Vincent Cocozza, was shot dead in a gangland

127

Although prone to obesity, Mario Lanza was mobbed by adoring women.

killing. The experience left a deep impression on his young mind and before long his parents decided to move out of the overcrowded family home. They rented a two-storey house in another part of the Italian quarter. Close by was a record shop, where Mario spent most of his pocket money on opera records. At fifteen he was a broad shouldered, husky youth and his street friends found it hard to understand his passionate commitment to classical music. But he had already confessed to his mother that he wanted to be a singer.

After listening to him, a well-known coach advised that professional training should be left until he was at least nineteen. Instead, he was placed in the hands of eighty-year-old language teacher Maestro Pellizon, who had to be carried up two flights of stairs to where the Cocozzas kept their piano in order that he could give Mario lessons in Italian, French, German and sight-reading.

By the time he was nineteen and at the end of his tuition with Pellizon, he had mastered his languages and could sight-read like a professional. That Christmas he was asked to sing the Bach-Gounod *Ave Maria* in church. His voice had matured. As the first notes poured from his throat the whole congregation was spellbound, his parents astounded. Word swiftly went round the Italian quarter that the Cocozza family had produced another Enrico Caruso.

For 18 months he studied with a teacher called Irene Williams, who took him to sing at the homes of some of Philadelphia's richest and most influential people, hoping to find a patron who would invest in his future. One evening, the great conductor Koussevitsky was among those listening. After the performance, the Maestro asked to see the young Italian and offered him a scholarship. Lanza was over the moon. It was just the kind of patronage he needed, and before long *Opera News* was hailing him as 'the find of the season'. Another fortunate meeting, this time with Maria Margelli, secretary to famous singer Ezio Pinza, took him a stage further. She declared he had 'the greatest voice I've ever heard'. She offered to pay for his lessons and to feed him, and encouraged him to fix his sights on the Metropolitan Opera in New York. He was not, however, destined for the 'Met' – but for Hollywood.

In December 1942, just when he was about to take another step forward in his career, Lanza was called up for the Army Air Force. Because of an old eye injury, he was assigned to 'limited service'. He was drafted into the Military Police and shipped out to Marfa Air Force Base, a semi-deserted, dusty camp on the Texas prairie. He was utterly miserable. The dust and dry heat affected his voice and no one could have imagined a more unlikely MP than this gregarious, fun-loving Italian. Fortunately, a talent scout, looking for performers for service shows, realized he was being wasted and rescued him.

While still in uniform, Lanza made the first of three encounters with show business giants that eventually propelled him to stardom. After singing in a Frank Loesser service show called *On the Beam*, which was a huge success, he was invited to join the cast of Moss Hart's huge production, *Winged Victory*, in New York. As a latecomer to the show, he was given a part in the chorus. One day, at a dress rehearsal, he decided to loosen up his voice with a few bars from *Celeste Aïda*. Moss Hart, sitting in the stalls, was electrified. 'Who the hell's that?' he shouted. Lanza came from behind the curtain and Hart leapt to his feet. 'I'd no idea such talent was hidden in the chorus. That young man has a future in this business, if he wants it.'

When Warner Brothers decided to film *Winged Victory* in Hollywood, Lanza went with the rest of the cast. By the time filming ended, every studio in town had heard of the handsome young tenor. Maria Margelli, still looking after his interests, went to see Jack Warner himself and took with her a recording that Lanza had made in New York. Warner, known as a very tough customer, thought he was listening to Caruso. When he learned that the owner of the voice was waiting on the other side of his door, he called him in immediately. Warner told Lanza he had the best voice he had ever heard. He would like to give him a contract. There was only one drawback. 'Your chest and shoulders are too big for the screen. You won't photograph well.' Nevertheless, he asked Lanza to see him again. Maybe something could be done.

In January 1945, the singer was given a medical discharge from the Army Air Force and, from that moment on, things moved swiftly. He met and married Betty Hicks, a dark, beautiful girl, sister of one of his army friends; RCA-Victor signed him up as a major new recording artist and Enrico Rosati, who had taught Gigli, took him under his wing. When he went on tour he played to packed houses.

Before long, Louis B. Mayer of MGM was asking to see him. One of the studio's largest sound stages was set up for his audition. Unlike Warner, Mayer did not hesitate. After looking closely at the dark, handsome Italian face and listening to the pure, soaring voice, he offered a seven-year film contract.

To everyone's dismay, Lanza's first screen test was a disaster. His broad chest looked enormous, out of proportion, and his curly hair, kinky. The first signs of a weight problem that would make his life a misery were beginning to show. The studio got to work on him. In the hands of Terry Robinson, a young physical fitness expert who became a good friend, Lanza shed pounds. The wardrobe department gave him suits that made him look narrower and the hairdressers smoothed out his hair. His second test was a great success and girls in the studio fought for copies of his 'stills'.

For his first picture, *That Midnight Kiss*, Mario Lanza was teamed with a lovely young singing star, Kathryn Grayson. The film was sentimental and told the story of an ex–GI truck driver who is hired to move a piano, discovers music and becomes an opera singer. As the publicity department at MGM liked this idea, it was adopted as the truth. In the first wave of major national publicity that went out in September 1939, Lanza was depicted as a singing 'truckie' who had found his voice by accident. He was twenty-seven and his life would never be the same again.

After the release of *That Midnight Kiss*, Lanza paid a visit to his home town, where streets were decorated in his honour and a procession, led by the Mayor, made its way to the house where he had been born. When he tried to leave his car to eat in a restaurant, the fans went mad. They tore his shirt collar, ripped buttons from his coat and pulled out lumps of his hair. 'I never want to face a mob like that again,' he told his wife; but it was only the beginning.

Wherever he went people called out, 'Sing, Mario! Sing!' and became offended if he tried to excuse himself. His records sold faster than his record company could produce them. Personal appearance tours began to make him nervous and his friend, Frank Sinatra, advised him to wear padding under his clothes as protection. Women drove up alongside him on Sunset Boulevard and screamed, 'Mario! Mario!' His fan mail, which the studio found increasing difficult to handle, brought blatant offers of sex from women of all ages. Young girls wrote saying they were on their way to Los Angeles and would kill themselves if he did not meet them at the train or bus terminal.

As fame and wealth increased, the Lanzas were invited to parties and receptions given by the richest people in Hollywood. Mario had always had a taste for extravagance, and the way *they* lived was the way he wanted to live. His personal manager, Sam Weiler, set up a corporation for him, into which his rapidly increasing income could be channelled for investments. It was operated from an elegant suite of offices in the Allen-Paris building in Beverly Hills. Meanwhile, the Lanza home in Whittier Drive became stuffed with costly antique furniture, rugs, pictures, foreign relics, anything that took the fancy of both Mario and Betty, who were compulsive buyers. There was also a fairytale nursery for their first baby daughter. Every Sunday was 'open house' at Whittier Drive, when the Lanzas would entertain 30 or 40 people at an all-day barbecue. Throngs of acquaintances dropped by at other times to sample their hospitality. Things became more and more frantic, until Mario and Betty were almost never alone.

Lanza's reputation soared with his next film *The Toast of New Orleans*, in which he sang the famous *Be My Love* as well as several operatic arias. The studio gave him a huge party to celebrate his twenty-eighth birthday during the shooting. Journalists were quick to notice how much he enjoyed his large slice of cake from the famous Sarno's bakery and he was desperately hurt next day when several columnists referred to him as 'the chubby tenor'. Alas, they had discovered his Achilles heel. Lanza had a natural tendency to put on weight and, like most Italians, relished pasta with rich sauces. His problem was made worse by the demands of MGM and his recording studio who, aware of the fact that an operatic tenor has a more resonant tone when he carries plenty of weight, allowed him to eat gargantuan meals while recording, but demanded that he slimmed down to look good for the cameras. As a result, his body metabolism was 'being manipulated like a yo-yo', say Lanza's biographers, Raymond Strait and Terry Robinson. It had the effect of making his behaviour erratic.

His career had taken off, and since he was always being compared with Caruso he knew it was only a matter of time before he was asked to play the rôle of the great tenor on screen. As it turned out, the filming of *The Great Caruso* was Lanza's greatest achievement. Singing with stars of the Metropolitan Opera, he was deeply moved when they rushed up to him after recording the sextet from *Lucia di Lammermoor* and urged him, 'Come to the "Met" . . . we need you at the "Met".'

Lanza had always insisted that he did not want to be regarded as a film star. First and foremost he was a singer. However, as the money rolled in, Hollywood took over. Blessed with an enormous zest for living, Mario went over the top. The Lanzas entertained lavishly, stayed up at all-night parties and breakfasted in bed in the late afternoon. Usually punctilious about being on the set on time, the singer began to miss rehearsals and was given a fatherly lecture by Louis B. Mayer. Betty was drinking too much and her behaviour provoked violent arguments that sometimes lasted, off and on, for weeks. When he could stand it no longer, Mario moved into the apartment provided for him on the MGM lot and usually found some pretty starlet to keep him company.

With the release of *The Great Caruso* album, which sold over a million copies, Lanza's career reached its peak. When he went on tour, so much money was made from ticket sales that it was referred to as 'The Lanza Bonanza'. As far as the studio and his recording company were concerned, he had become *very* big business.

Emotional chaos reigned in his personal life. To escape Betty's demands upon him and the fights – which were becoming more and more frequent, with lamps, vases and pieces of furniture used as missiles – Lanza sought distraction outside the home. He ate and drank too much and, when not actually filming, sometimes gorged himself to the point of physical pain. Women, nevertheless, found him devastatingly attractive, swarmed around him and offered themselves to him as consolation. Sometimes, he would promise a girl he had known for only a few hours a part in one of his films and send her away loaded with expensive presents and money.

Part of this was just his Latin zest for living and loving, but his friends suspected he also had difficulty in knowing how to handle so much money, so much fame. 'Success had come too easily and too soon,' wrote his biographers Strait and Robinson in *Lanza, His Tragic Life.* 'He didn't have time to learn the restraint that ten more years of struggle might have taught him. He wasn't prepared for the constant insecurity of being a star.'

As long as the awards and plaudits kept coming, Lanza was happy enough. He was thrilled when *The Great Caruso* was announced Top Film of the Year in London, and when this was followed by RCA-Victor releasing the news that his recording of *The Loveliest Night of the Year* had won him a second gold disc, he decided to celebrate in style.

At the time, he was filming *Because You're Mine* with the exquisite soprano, Doretta Morrow. Everyone connected with the film was invited to the party, believed to be the most lavish ever given on an MGM set. Everyone received a gold watch with a special engraving, and even gatecrashers walked off with expensive mementoes. Dore Schary, who had taken over top production at MGM, was not amused. The chemistry between the two men was not good. Schary had – wrongly, it so happens – predicted that Lanza's second film, *The Toast of New Orleans*, would turn out to be 'a lemon'. Now Lanza was getting his own back. On set he had been behaving like a spoilt child, throwing tantrums, refusing to diet then going on hunger strike; now this crazy party! When Schary was reported to have said he was losing patience, Lanza retorted, 'I'll worry about him when I stop making money.'

Lanza knew his value to MGM. *The Great Caruso* had pulled in $19 million in less than a year and now, as a reward, he was offered *The Student Prince*, a highly romantic story that he felt was tailor-made for him. In his personal life things were more settled. Betty was expecting their second child and they had moved into a magnificent mansion in Bel Air, where Mario had a music room and a gymnasium. Everything looked set for a wonderful future.

Rumours that MGM were having trouble with their temperamental star began to circulate soon after *The Student Prince* started production. Director, Furtis Bernhardt, it was said, had tried to persuade Lanza to tone down his high-powered, emotional singing style for the part. Lanza was incensed that he, of all people, should be told how to sing and demanded that a new director be brought in. When the studio refused, he walked off the set and disappeared for several days.

He returned to find he had been suspended. This meant that not only was he off salary at the studio but, under the terms of his contract, he could not take other work. When Schary, who had been ordering daily reports on Lanza's behaviour, told him these conditions, the screaming and yelling could be heard all over the set.

After the interview with Schary, Lanza, in a furious temper, announced that he would not be making *The Student Prince*. MGM's answer came like a thunderbolt. The studio sued for almost $700 000 in special damages, plus $4.5 million in general damages. They claimed it would cost that much to abandon the film. To make matters worse, the government was also demanding payment of back taxes. Lanza suddenly realized that unless he did something to correct the situation, his lavish lifestyle would go down the drain. He had made so much money in his short career that the prospect did not seem real. The idea of 'cutting back' appalled him. With Betty installed in a house in Palm Springs awaiting the birth of their third child, he decided to mend his fences with MGM. Eventually, *The Student Prince* was made, with Lanza's voice pouring from the throat of the handsome young actor Edmund Purdom.

At the end of 1954, Warner Brothers asked Lanza to make *Serenade* for them, promising to borrow the great Licia Albenese from the 'Met' to sing with him. All the omens were good. Lanza's voice had never been better; his drinking was under control and he was full of good humour on the set, often doing hilarious impressions of Liberace or Nat King Cole before launching into an aria. But when the film moved out of the studio and on to location in a small town called San Miguel de Allende, in Mexico, things started to go wrong. Lanza was mobbed by his Mexican fans, but the adulation did nothing to stem the dark tide of self-destruction that was stirring in him again.

Soon, the making of *Serenade* became a nightmare. Hypersensitive about his weight, he trusted nobody and complained that all anyone cared about was 'The Voice'. The old temperamental Lanza was back. Worst of all he discovered the fiery, potent Mexican drink, tequila. After drinking a whole bottle one night he seduced a young Mexican girl and, in order to avoid a scandal, the studio had to pay compensation to her family and hastily remove their star.

His answer to all the demons that plagued him was to spend money more recklessly than ever. This led to his first contact with the Mafia.

One of the singer's greatest admirers was boxer Rocky Marciano, who realized that Lanza was dissipating his wealth and would soon be in financial deep water. One day, Rocky paid him a visit with two 'friends'. One of them was a Mr Lucchese, better known to the underworld as 'Three Fingers Brown', close friend and confidant of infamous Mafia boss 'Lucky' Luciano. According to Lanza's biographers, Lucchese made an offer to take charge of the singer's career. Then, he assured him, all his financial troubles would be over. Lanza, who wanted nothing to do with the Mafia, was very drunk and showed his would-be promoter to the door with four-letter-word contempt. Lucchese turned on the singer like a cobra, called him 'a fat slob', and warned him he had made a big mistake.

Lanza's agents and his business managers thought it would be a good idea for the singer to spend a few years in Europe. He had millions of fans over there and MGM came up with an attractive film proposition. Shooting would begin in Rome in May 1957. One friend who saw Mario and Betty off made a shrewd observation. 'They were different from the couple I used to know. Older, of course, but there was something else. They were different inside. The life they'd led had done something to them.'

On the outside, things looked good. The Lanzas rented the palatial Villa Badoglio, once owned by Mussolini. It was furnished throughout with French and Italian antiques and the surrounding estate had swimming pools, tennis courts and enough garage space for Mario's fleet of cars. The children were in a separate wing with their nannies and governesses.

Lanza felt that he was starting life afresh and could leave all the bitterness of Hollywood behind him. There were two triumphant visits to London. On the first trip, he was given top billing at the Royal Variety Performance and introduced to Queen Elizabeth. On the second visit, he sang to a packed Albert Hall at three sell-out concerts.

Behind the great doors of the Villa Badoglio, however, the old demons were catching up. Mario was living life to the hilt again, spending money like water and ignoring his doctor's advice about diet and alcohol. Though he was only thirty-eight, he was being treated for diabetes, gout and phlebitis. And his temper had an unfortunately short fuse.

One day he lost his temper with, of all people, Lucky Luciano. The Mafia boss had been deported to Italy from the United States and called on Lanza with a business proposition. The singer had always been gregarious and couldn't help being interested in the notorious gangster. When Luciano began talking about 'a deal', however, the temperature began to rise. Lanza's mother, on a visit to see her grandchildren, was appalled when she heard Luciano and her son yelling at each other. Before she returned to America she told him: 'Stay away from people like Luciano . . . you don't need him around your house or your children.'

Luciano gradually wore the singer down until, as a concession, he agreed to do just one charity performance in Naples; but no more. When Betty found out she was appalled, knowing that the demands would not end there. Mario, too, knew he had made a grave error but did not know how to extricate himself.

Instead of turning up at rehearsals for Luciano's charity concert, Lanza signed himself into a clinic on the pretext of getting treatment for his gout and phlebitis, which had seriously begun to affect one leg. He was put on a new method of weight-reducing that involved intravenous injections of urine from pregnant women. He hated needles and rang home from his hospital bed to complain. Betty told him to relax and follow doctors' orders.

She was desperately worried. Mario should never have agreed to do the concert if he had not meant to go through with it. 'This isn't MGM you're walking out on,' she warned him.

No one knows exactly how Mario Lanza died. A doctor phoned Betty to say he had developed a bad heart; a nurse then contradicted him by calling to say it was pneumonia. Lanza, himself, was obviously worried and protested he was as strong as a bull, apart from his leg, and wanted to go home. But on 7 October 1959, he went into a coma from which he never recovered. His chauffeur found him unattended with a needle still deeply embedded in his arm, a rubber tube leading to an empty bottle.

Betty Lanza, almost out of her mind with grief, cried: 'I think the Mafia had something to do with it. I think they murdered Mario.' His body was taken back to Hollywood for a funeral attended by the great and famous and members of his own deeply distressed family. Betty did not live much longer and was buried alongside him in Holy Cross Cemetery.

Chapter Six

WHO WANTS TO BE A BILLIONAIRE?

Men whose dream it is to make money . . . who live and breathe money, and who end their days in a nightmare of barren loneliness.

'A rich person ought to have a strong stomach.'

Walt Whitman

Alfried Krupp

On the morning of Wednesday, 11 April 1945, the victorious American 9th Army set up a command post in the area of Essen on the German Ruhr. Two officers, one of them a colonel, were sent to make enquiries at the great Gothic mansion they had seen on the outskirts of the industrial city.

They marched into the gloomy, vaulted entrance hall of the Villa Hügel to be met by the chief butler.

'Who lives here?' barked the Colonel.

The German servant, who in his time had dealt with the Kaiser, the Führer and the Duce replied icily, 'My master, Dilomingenieur Alfried Krupp von Bohlen und Halbach.'

'Where is he?'

'Upstairs.'

'Bring him down at once.'

When Krupp did not appear the Colonel, gun in hand, brushed the butler aside and rushed upstairs. In a second-floor bedroom he found a tall, slender man immaculately dressed in a pin-striped suit, calmly adjusting his tie in a mirror.

'I am the owner of the property. What do you want?'

'You are under arrest.'

Without more ceremony Alfried Krupp, head of the vast German armaments firm, whose father had made a pact with Hitler, was seized and bundled into the back of a jeep. He was about to be made to pay the price for the vast fortune his family had made out of the weapons of death, and for their active part in the German war machine.

Alfried Krupp, himself, felt that the whole weight of the family's guilt had been laid at his door and when, two years after his arrest, he was brought before the judges at the Nuremberg war trials, he pleaded that he was being persecuted because of the dynasty's reputation, and that he had been condemned merely by accident of birth.

But nothing could explain away the fact that the Krupp family had been fully committed to the Nazi party and that Alfried's father, old Gustav, now a helpless wreck of a man struck down by illness, had worshipped Hitler

Alfried Krupp von Bohlen und Halbach at the Villa Hügel.

and had used slave labour in his munitions factories. As a dutiful son, Alfried said, he had had no option but to follow in his father's footsteps.

He was a pale, austere figure as he sat stiff and erect in the seat previously occupied by Hermann Göring at Nuremberg. The judges listened to everything; then gave him a 12-year sentence and confiscated all his property. The Allies were determined to crush the Krupp empire for ever. Visibly shaken, Alfried was led away to begin paying the price – in a solitary cell with a tin bucket.

No one dreamed that he would be released after six years, that the Krupp empire would rise again, like a phoenix from the ashes; that Alfried would turn from arms manufacturer to one of the world's largest producers of steel and coal; that the Villa Hügel would be made into an art centre.

Alfried, it was true, had inherited a terrible legacy. The Krupps first came to the attention of the world in 1851 when Alfried's great-grandfather, Alfred, presented the new Krupp steel cannon at the Great Exhibition in Crystal Palace, London. The gun caused a sensation, because all the guns in use up to that time were made of brass. By 1887, Krupp had sold over 250 000 of them to 21 nations. He was known throughout the world as 'The Cannon King'.

As his power increased, megalomania set in. Alfred was a benevolent despot, who would look after his workers from the cradle to the grave; but, in return, he demanded total allegiance. He built the cavernous, gloomy Villa Hügel as a suitably impressive headquarters for the dynasty, but it was a doomed house that never brought happiness to anyone who lived in it. There, he entertained great industrialists, cabinet ministers, princes, and even the Kaiser. But he ended his life there a bitter old man, riddled with fear, wandering from room to room, because he believed if he stayed in one too long the air would become foul and kill him.

Though he despised his semi-invalid son Friedrich, when he died in 1887 it was he who succeeded him and, in his own quiet way, kept the firm together. To Friedrich and his wife Margarethe was born a daughter, Bertha, who grew up to be a stately, rather formidable young lady. A true German aristocrat, she married just the right sort of man to sire the Krupp heirs – Gustav von Bohlen und Halbach, Prussian diplomat at the Vatican. On Friedrich's death the empire passed into the hands of the two women, Margarethe and Bertha, but when Bertha married Gustav in 1906 he took over the responsibility.

Alfried was born on 13 August 1907 and was given the name Krupp. His christening took place at the Villa Hügel at a lavish ceremony attended by the Kaiser. The year of his birth was considered auspicious, for it coincided with the launching of the first U-boat, regarded at the time as a triumph of German engineering, and also with the opening of the Krupps' first electric steel plant.

All the Krupp children were brought up with what Gustav considered real German efficiency. He imposed a life of almost monastic severity upon them. Though the villa was furnished with almost claustrophobic luxury, the heating was kept at a minimum, to save fuel and discourage sloth. Meals were frugal when there were no guests present and, by all accounts, there was little enjoyment or fun.

As son and heir, Alfried was singled out for special attention. From early childhood, his father drummed into him that self-discipline, self-restraint and single-mindedness were of paramount importance. He was taught French before he spoke German, as French was the language of international affairs. He spent most of his day with teachers and servants, who were instructed to report to Gustav any sign of disobedience.

There was little love or laughter at the Villa Hügel, especially after the outbreak of the First World War in 1914. All that mattered then was to meet the needs of the German war machine. At the height of the conflict, the crucible steel plant alone was employing some 115 000 men. Gustav was thought to have made profits in the region of £40 million.

Alfried was twelve when he was taken to see the awe-inspiring industrial empire that he would one day take over. Educated at home by private tutors, he had little knowledge of what was going on in the world outside the Villa Hügel. He had no idea, for instance, that the very name of Krupp was hated throughout most of Europe, that it had become synonymous with death.

At the end of the First World War the Allies dismantled the Krupp plant, swearing that it would 'never rise again'. But after a few years, a peace-time compromise was reached. Krupps would be allowed to start production again, provided they built only trains, trucks and tractors, instead of weapons of death. Alfried started his apprenticeship in the post-war plant.

He rode to the works each morning on a motor scooter, punched his time card and, at the end of the day, collected a meagre wage packet. When he had had experience of every department, he was sent first to Munich, then to other universities to study science and technology. He revelled in the freedom and developed a passion for high-speed motoring. To complete his education, he spent six months in 1935 as an unpaid employee at a bank in Berlin.

Unfortunately, Alfried had become a problem. He was starting to enjoy himself. Bored with work in the Dresdner Bank in Berlin, he spent a brief period, never to be enjoyed again, as an international playboy. He was seen in Cannes, Nice and Estoril in a gleaming sports car and in the company of pretty, frivolous girls. As William Manchester says in his definitive book on the family, *The Arms of Krupp*, the spree was brief, and perhaps it was also pitiful. Before the winter of 1935, he was back in the Ruhr. For the rest of his life he would be shackled to responsibility.

On one thing, however, Alfried would not give way. He had met and fallen in love with Anneliese Bahr, the quiet fair-haired daughter of a Hamburg importer, and was determined to marry her. His father was against the marriage, because she was not the type of girl who fitted in with the great Krupp women, 'valkyries' like Margarethe and Bertha. His mother objected, because Anneliese had been married before. But for once, Alfried went against family wishes and, on 11 November, 1937, made Anneliese his wife. Their only son, Arndt, was born the following year.

Alfried's parents continued to regard their son's marriage as morganatic, and when Gustav discovered, through discreet inquiries, that Anneliese's sister had married a Jew, it was the last straw. The Krupps froze the girl out of the family. Once it was seen that she was not accepted at the Villa Hügel, she was rejected everywhere. In the end, the unhappy couple gave way and separated. After the divorce Alfried withdrew more deeply into himself, his eyes grew colder and his manner more impersonal.

Just before his marriage, Alfried had been formally installed as director of the firm of Friedrich Krupp. Gustav was fully committed to the National Socialist Party, and his son saw no option but to go along with his father. He did not, however, become a full member of the Nazi party until the end of 1938.

It was now the eve of the Second World War. Gustav was prepared to start making armaments as soon as possible, and he thrust Alfried to the forefront of the German war effort. Alfried was now thirty-two, and the former playboy had become very serious about his rôle. Once again the Krupps would play their full part in total war.

Gustav was content to leave the rôle of 'Cannon King' to his son and, in 1943, Alfried took over as head of all Krupp enterprises. By the age of thirty-six he had reached a pinnacle of position, wealth and power. He was able to supply Hitler with all the armaments he needed by using slave labour – the desperate, half-starved workers brought from the concentration camps Hitler had established.

But, by the Summer of 1944, all the dreams of glory, of glittering prizes that would come to the Krupps as a result of the war, suddenly began to fade. British, American and Free French troops were already on their way to liberate Europe. Day after day, the air raids on Essen became more intensive. The Krupp works were a principal target for the Allies, but Alfried kept working as the bombs rained down. On 11 March 1945, Essen suffered its last and worst air raid. More than one third of the main Krupp factory was demolished and production came to a halt. As the war reached its final stages, Alfried knew he would be brought to account. It was a month later that the two American officers came and arrested Alfried at the Villa Hügel.

After his sentence at the Nuremberg trials – his face went chalk white when he heard the Krupp plant was to be confiscated – he was sent to be imprisoned at the ancient fortress of Landsberg, in Bavaria. The mighty Krupp now had to slop out, wash dishes, wash clothes and work in the blacksmith's shop, like any common prisoner. But the rigid self-control he had learned in childhood served him now. He never allowed anyone to know what he was thinking or feeling.

Whilst in prison, Krupp conceived the idea of restoring the Krupp empire; but this time, for peaceful purposes and under the umbrella of Marshall Aid, the great American scheme for rebuilding Europe. America was willing to lend its support to anyone who could contribute to the economic development of the country and to the stability of Europe. Krupp's willingness to help was made known to both the American and British authorities and, on 3 February 1951, along with twenty-eight other prisoners, he was freed in an amnesty.

Within a week, he was back at Essen, walking through the ruins of the empire he had inherited. He was greeted like a returning hero by his workers. But not everyone was glad to see him free, and when he tried to return to the Villa Hügel, he encountered a sign ten feet high reading: No Visitors – Except on Official Business.

Krupp realized his best defence was extreme discretion. For the first two years of his new freedom, his whereabouts were unknown for weeks at a time. He concentrated on his private life, and in May 1952, at the age of forty-five, married for a second time. Fraulein Vera Hossenfeldt was a completely new experience – beautiful, petite, with a heart-shaped face, a stunning figure and no inhibitions. She was a member of the new jet set, previously married three times. To avoid comment, they slipped away to a registrar's office in the Bavarian mountain resort of Berchtesgaden and were married secretly.

Now he was determined to put the past behind him. Nothing would have persuaded him to move back into the Villa Hügel and he decided to 'leave it to the ghosts'. He built a new villa for his attractive wife, just outside Essen, and moved quietly into society again, not too sure of the reception he would get.

The story of his phoenix-like rise is famous.

Stripped of his coal and steel interests, he created the Krupp consulting engineering department, which sent out teams of mining engineers, geologists, steel experts and machine fitters to every part of the world. His most unlikely partner in this new enterprise was an extrovert, one-time bank clerk and insurance executive, Berthold Beitz, an extraordinary, self-made man who was mad about jazz and used American slang. Under Krupp, Beitz became the sole administrator of a business empire whose total assets were in the neighbourhood of £400 million.

In November 1954, Alfred Krupp gave a reception in honour of the Emperor of Ethiopia. Five hundred guests were invited, including 120 diplomats who were driven from Bonn in black Mercedes limousines. At the banquet, stuffed lobster, foie gras and black caviar was served on gold plate. Bertha Krupp stood regally beside her son to receive the guests. The beautiful Vera was nowhere in sight. Bored with her life as a Krupp she had fled to America, where gossip columnists reported seeing her in New York society and bathing in the California sun.

The divorce action was cold and bitter. As *The Manchester Guardian* commented at the time: 'As he saw his wealth building up once more to Kruppian heights, so the curse that seemed to exist along with the Krupp money was at work again.' Vera complained that he was always immersed in his work, that his relations ignored her. 'I value my freedom in America more than all his money,' she told reporters.

Although there seemed to be no end to Krupp's post-war success, he looked a gaunt, unhappy figure, and after the death of his mother in 1957, was obviously a lonely man, a compulsive worker with many aquaintances but few close friends.

News of his death, on 30 July 1967, shocked most people. One spokesman issued a Press release describing it as 'sudden and unexpected'. But a further bulletin disclosed he had been suffering from an incurable disease, probably lung cancer caused by smoking. He was buried with great splendour, and with him too the old order of Krupp. Alfried's son, Arndt, had no desire to reign over the Ruhr. He preferred the exotic pleasures of the jet set and the French riviera.

John D. Rockefeller

One of the richest men the world has ever known, John D. Rockefeller, founder of Standard Oil, lived for part of his life on a diet of milk and biscuits and went to his local Baptist church twice on Sundays. His children did not dare to leave a scrap of food on their plates or a light burning when they left the room. He was depicted in newspaper cartoons as a narrow-lipped zealot handing out dimes to the deserving poor.

Considered by many to be an unrepentant sinner who had made his money by ruthlessly trampling over others, John Davison Rockefeller was hated in his day. Hundreds used to gather to watch him lead his family into church on Sundays – 'as if to witness the passing of a camel through the eye of a needle.'

Strange, then, that the name of Rockefeller would eventually be revered as the source of one of the greatest systems of philanthropy the world has ever known.

The first John D. Rockefeller was a serious, secret man with cold, shrewd eyes and a humourless slit of a mouth. As a young man he did not seem to enjoy life and did not see why anyone else should. Making money became an obsession he could not control, but he convinced himself that, as a pillar of the church, he was paving his way to heaven.

When his fortune became so vast he didn't know what to do with it, he was talked into giving large chunks of it away for charitable purposes, in order to perpetuate the family name. By the time he died, he had given away millions of dollars. He usually insisted on naming his own terms. For instance, when a large donation went to rebuild the University of Chicago, he insisted that the new University should be 'aggressively Christian with no infidel teachers'!

He came originally from thrifty, hardworking farming stock. The first Rockefeller, Johann Peter, had arrived in America from Germany in 1723 and his family gradually spread across New York State and Pennsylvania. John D. was born on 8 July 1839, in an isolated farmhouse ringed by apple trees, and two hours drive from the nearest hamlet of Richford in western New York.

The mean John D. Rockefeller became an emaciated old man.

His father, William, was different from most of the Rockefellers. Though successful in farming, he made his money as a seller of patent medicines and potions. 'Doc' Rockefeller, as he was known, was a character larger than life. Over six feet tall, he had bright blue eyes and a ginger beard, and dressed in fine worsted suiting with a brocaded waistcoat. He had a healthy distrust of bankers and kept bundles of money in a hayloft, tied with string. He was away from the homestead much of the time, peddling his quack cures to gullible country folk. Moreover, William had a secret. For forty years, he had been leading a double life: in South Dakota he was known as Dr William Levingston, and was bigamously married to a woman twenty years younger than himself.

John did not resemble his father in any way. The boy took after his mother Eliza, a thin, hatchet-faced prude who had married Bill Rockefeller in an uncharacteristic fit of passion. He inherited from her a narrow, almost expressionless face, hooded eyes and thin lips. Her pious, Calvinist sayings, especially 'Woeful waste makes woeful want', stayed with him all his life.

He had acute money sense from the earliest age. When he was only seven, he managed to raise a flock of turkeys by watching a wild hen's nest, then taking her brood as it hatched. He raised the poults and sold them for a good profit. At about the same time, he began to save coins in a china bowl, which his mother placed on a chest in the living-room. Within three years, he had enough money to lend a neighbouring farmer $50 at seven per cent interest. When the money was returned a year later, with $3.50 interest, he was impressed. It was more than he had made in ten days hard work hoeing potatoes. From that day on, young John vowed he would make money work for him.

By the time he was fourteen, his family had moved to Cleveland, Ohio, and he went to the Central High School, where his dour features earned him the nickname of 'The Deacon'. Asked what he wanted to be when he grew up he replied, precociously, 'I want to be worth a hundred thousand dollars, and I *will* be too.'

Rockefeller started his career as a four–dollars–a–week clerk-accountant, with a firm of commission merchants and produce shippers. He would be at his desk by 6.30 every morning, and worked with utter dedication. Apart from going to church, he had no other interests. Every penny he spent was written down in a little black book.

By 1858, when he was nineteen and still working with the same firm, he was earning $600 a year. But he reckoned he was worth more. When his employers refused to increase his wages, he decided the time had come to work for himself. He had got to know a young Englishman, called Maurice Clark, who worked for another firm of commission agents in Cleveland,

and suggested to him that they should go into business together. John borrowed some money from his father and agreed to pay him ten per cent interest.

The partnership of Clark and Rockefeller flourished. In the first year they made a profit of $4000, but with the outbreak of the American Civil War, in 1861, commodity prices rose sharply and orders came pouring in. Rockefeller gained a reputation as one of the shrewdest dealers in town. In a world full of conmen, he let it be known that *nobody* was going to take him for a ride.

All the time he was dealing in commodities, Rockefeller was fully aware that men were making fortunes in oil. But he knew in his bones that the *real* money would be made not at the pump, but in the middle-man stages of hauling and refining. The time was not quite ripe. Transportation was still uncertain, and refining processes too crude. He would wait.

He became engaged to a pious, grave, pretty young woman called Laura Spelman. It was said he had pursued her with dogged determination and once he had made up his mind, no one else would do. They were married on 8 September 1864. Rockefeller made a note under 'sundry expenses' in his accounts book – 'One wedding ring: 15 dollars 75 cents.'

Once he had convinced himself the oil around Cleveland was not going to dry up, John D. began to transfer his attention from the commission business to refining. Buying out his partners on the crest of an oil boom, he started on the road that would lead him to untold wealth. A startled bystander watched one day as, thinking himself alone in the office, he jumped into the air, clicked his heels together and repeated: 'I'm bound to be rich! Bound to be rich! *Bound to be rich!*'

Telling the complex Rockefeller story in *An American Dynasty*, American writers Peter Collier and David Horowitz say that, from then on, John D. poured his passion and his genius into the creation of Standard Oil, leaving his life as dry as old bones. Though he had no conception of the industrial giant he would create, he knew he was on to something enormous. His methods of doing business, however, made him many bitter enemies.

In a three-months' *blitzkrieg*, he bought out all but three of his 25 competitors in Cleveland. Small businessmen had no chance. He just wiped them out. People were stunned to realize that his Standard Oil Company soon had the city's refining capacity sewn up. By 1880, Rockefeller was refining 95 per cent of the oil produced across the entire nation. He had just about cornered the market.

Rich beyond his wildest dreams, John D. decided to acquire a house for his growing family that would reflect their status in the world. He bought a rambling 700-acre estate at Forest Hill, with an equally rambling house,

house, ornate with turrets, towers, verandahs and masses of scrolled ironwork. He loved the place, but could not abandon the idea that somehow it could be turned into profit. Four years after buying it, he hired extra staff and tried to run it as a hotel for paying guests. Friends invited to Forest Hill for the weekend were astonished to receive a bill when they returned home. Finally, the idea was dropped.

Though in business Rockefeller was regarded as a tyrant – 'a great spider sitting back in his web seeking whom he may destroy' – he was a devoted family man. His children worshipped him, but grew up completely unaware that they belonged to the richest family in Cleveland. All four of them did chores to earn pocket money and kept daily accounts of every cent they spent.

Within John D's offices, a degree of sanctimonious decorum was enforced, which many found hard to comply with. His staff had to dress and conduct themselves as though they were attending a deacons' meeting. He was constantly on the prowl with his little black book, and his workers never knew when he would appear beside them to complain about some 'extravagance' or other. Drink was taboo. At one time John Archbold, the executive who would one day head Standard Oil, was talked into taking a pledge of temperance by his boss. He had to report to him once a month, like a criminal on parole. Archbold, who found it hard to abandon the bottle, took to whistling *Onward Christian Soldiers* in the corridor and carried a supply of cloves to sweeten his breath.

Rockefeller shunned the other great industrialists who were beginning to make their mark towards the end of the last century. He did not mix with them socially. He was appalled at the way so many of his fellow multi-millionaires threw their money around on frivolities, such as yachts, jewels, parties and women. (Social commentator Lucius Beebe says no Rockefeller on record is ever known to have had a good time.)

Gradually the tentacles of Standard Oil extended across whole continents. Rockefeller, himself, believed he had built up an organization that had benefited the world – and in many ways he was right. But he had also become associated with acts of ruthlessness in his rise to pre-eminence, and there were many people who would never forget it. It was said that, at one time, towards the end of the last century, hatred clung to him like iron filings to a magnet. By 1902, the feeling was so strong that he began receiving death threats and slept with a revolver under his pillow.

Standard Oil was now so big that it encompassed 40 corporations. Rockefeller decided, regretfully, that he would have to uproot his family from Cleveland, where they had lived so long, and establish his headquarters at the heart of the business world, in New York. He bought a fashionable Fifth Avenue house and set up the new corporate offices at 26 Broadway. His own sanctum there was almost spartan.

In public he remained austerely calm, but those closest to him saw that he was beginning to show strain. His days were now dominated by the endless manipulation of income and expenses, of investments, corporate strategy and legal matters. Fantastic dividends poured in, but people were beginning to wonder whether he was the master of his money, or vice versa.

After 40 years of wheeling and dealing, John D's body was beginning to fail him. His biographers say, to begin with, people thought his conscience was troubling him at the thought of meeting his God in the face of the hatred he had earned. But, as time went by, they realized he had not a scrap of remorse or reflective torment. He suffered from insomnia and paced the house at night. His stomach played up. He had to cut out the juicy steaks he was partial to, and live on milk and crackers. His face became deeply lined and he lost all his hair. In an uncharacteristic touch of vanity, he first hid his baldness with a black skull-cap, but later appeared in a series of ill-fitting white wigs.

His doctor advised him to change his lifestyle, to slow down; his public relations men advised him to change his image, to give to charity and deserving causes some of the money that came pouring into the Rockefeller coffers day after day. His son, John D. Rockefeller II also did his best to persuade his father to 'open up the family purse'.

Rockefeller's attitude to money had always been coloured by the thrift conscious teachings of his mother. He was not ungenerous to his employees, but he didn't give much away. His biographers tell the story of one of the army of groundkeepers at Pocantino, the house to which he retired. The groundkeeper was given a 5-dollar bill as a Christmas bonus, only to have it docked for spending the holiday with his wife and children instead of at work. None of the Rockefeller employees had national holidays off. John D. explained: 'Instead of spending money on amusements, they will be given the opportunity of adding to their savings. Had they been given a holiday, no doubt their money would have been spent foolishly.'

When presented with the idea of philanthropy on a grander scale, however, Rockefeller was more interested. He had always given to the Baptist church – millions it was said, in piecemeal donations – and his money had gone to rebuild Chicago University. Perhaps now was the time to soften the public attitude towards him. He decided to become a munificent benefactor.

He slowly began to relax his grip on Standard Oil. In 1897 he stopped going to the New York office and kept in touch only by telephone. The magnificent estate he had bought, located in the Pocantino Hills, overlooking the Hudson River, occupied him now. There, he built a spectacular golf course and, when he was not toying with the stock market, spent his life on the green. Standard Oil had been his one great passion. He was not interested in books, music or ideas and, like fellow tycoon John Ford, believed that thinking 'mussed up the mind'.

Plans for great philanthropic schemes went ahead, and in spite of their initial scepticism that old John D. meant well, his fellow Americans could not help but be mightily impressed. As many of the contemporaries, who had regarded him as the devil incarnate, faded away he was looked upon as just mildly eccentric. With the passing of the years he began to relax a little, and even produced the occasional wry joke. Once, while having a massage, he heard the creaking in his bones. He muttered under his breath: 'All the oil in the country, they say, and not enough to oil my own joints.'

Though he had taken to handing out coins to any children he saw in the street, he was not particularly interested in how his millions were being spent on charitable causes. He was quite content to leave the details to his son and other trustees. However, in 1913 the Rockefeller Foundation was finally given its charter and, true to his promise, John D. put aside $100 million for the institution, 'to promote the well being of mankind throughout the world.'

The last 20 years or so of his life were spent in gentle routine, every minute of his day accounted for. He seemed to shrink with the passing years and, by the time he reached his 90s, weighed less than 100 pounds.

If Rockefeller had one ambition left, it was to live to be a hundred. But it was not to be. On 23 May 1937, when he was ninety-eight, he failed to get up for morning prayers. His son was sent for, but by the afternoon he sank into a coma from which he never emerged.

At the moment he was lowered into his grave, Standard Oil employees all over the world stopped work for five minutes. He may not have approved of that. But the man who had once been loathed was now regarded as a benefactor of mankind.

Aristotle Onassis

W hen he was in the prime of his life and it began to seem as though his money could buy *anything*, they called Aristotle Onassis 'The Golden Greek'. The tough, charismatic shipping magnate created a world where his power was formidable and in which he ruled like some Byzantine emperor.

Onassis owned an island like a demi-paradise, a yacht like a floating palace, half of Monaco, an airline, beautiful houses – and beautiful women. His first wife was shipping heiress, Tina Livanos; his second, Jackie Kennedy; and for years he had a passionate affair with operatic superstar, Maria Callas. To crown all his achievements, there were two sturdy children to carry on his name.

No wonder he seemed like some character in Greek tragedy when, towards the end of his life, the gods began to demand payment for bestowing their gifts so liberally. The fantastic fortune he had amassed could not hold back the blows of fate. They did not cease with his death, either, for in November 1988 Christina, the daughter he had loved and who inherited his fortune, was found dead in Buenos Aires at the house of a friend. She was only thirty-eight but in the throes of divorce from her fourth husband and fighting a losing battle with her weight. There was talk of an overdose, swiftly denied. She left behind a three-year-old daughter, Athina, who will one day inherit the Onassis millions.

Those who met him sensed the drama in 'Ari' Onassis. It had been there from the very beginning. Though the myth makers would have him born poor, he was, in fact, the son of one of the richest tobacco merchants in the Greek quarter of Smyrna, on the west coast of Turkey. Born on 20 January 1906, he was an unruly child, but clever. He had a natural talent for languages but his father warned him: 'Great scholars do not make good businessmen and are seldom rich. As a teenager, conscious of his below-average height, and determined to develop a splendid physique, he became a keen swimmer, oarsman and water polo player.

But the idyllic days on the beaches of the eastern Mediterranean came to an end in the summer of 1922 when the war, that had been raging between Greeks and Turks in the interior, reached Smyrna. Turkish troops turned the city into a bloodbath. Young Aristotle lost half his family and his father,

'Ari' Onassis had a certain charismatic style, irresistible to women.

Socrates, was taken to a concentration camp. Only the sharp wit, daring and bravado of sixteen-year-old Ari saved the rest of the family and eventually won the freedom of his father. With the family savings bandaged to his body, he managed to gather his family together on the mainland of Greece to start a new life.

Ari was deeply hurt by his father's attitude towards his bravery. Far from being grateful, Socrates was only concerned about how much money had been rescued from the family safe in Smyrna. Finally, the young man decided he had done his duty and would find his future elsewhere. On 27 August 1923 Aristotle Onassis boarded the emigrant ship *Tomaso di Savoya* bound for Argentina. He had the equivalent of £62 sewn inside his jacket lining.

In Buenos Aires, young Aristotle was just one of thousands of refugees seeking work and, to begin with, he took anything that came along. Night shifts as a telephonist lifted him into a slightly higher income bracket and left him free during the day to pursue his new business venture. The tobacco trade was booming, women were beginning to smoke and he had access, through his father, to fragrant, oriental blends. He began to make a luxurious, gold tipped cigarette and to import tobaccco. Within a few years, by using a mixture of bluff, charm, determination and tough dealing, Aristotle had built up a prosperous tobacco business which made him a dollar millionaire.

Still, he was not satisfied. He was only too aware that the shipping companies who transported his tobacco were making more money than he was. Shipping, he decided, was the business to be in. When he heard that the Canadian National Steamship Company was in trouble and had ten freighters laid up in the St Lawrence River available at $30 000 each, he employed a marine engineer and set off for Canada. The price of the freighters, he knew, was rock bottom and barely above scrap value. At the end of three days, during which he personally examined each ship in detail, he said he would take six of them if the price was dropped to $20 000. As nobody else seemed to want them, the Canadians reluctantly agreed. Onassis had taken his first step towards becoming the most famous shipowner in the world.

Though his passion was business, Onassis knew how to enjoy himself. Women found him attractive, slightly mysterious, and a little threatening – a potent cocktail. But he also knew how to make them laugh. He had many affairs during the 1930s, the most important, which lasted for five years, with a Garbo-esque Scandinavian called Ingeborg Dedichen. But he was waiting for the real prize.

Onassis was first introduced to Athina, younger daughter of immensely wealthy Greek shipowner Stravros Livanos when she was only fourteen. But he knew immediately that he wanted her for his wife and was prepared to wait. Three years later, when she had developed into a delicate beauty with pale gold hair and wide brown eyes, he began to court her with old world courtesy. When he formally asked Livanos for her hand in marriage, he was refused. Livanos thought Aristotle should have asked for his eldest daughter, Eugenie; it was considered unseemly in orthodox Greek families for the younger daughter to be married first. Tina's evident unhappiness at this led Livanos to change his mind. Ari and Tina were married at the Greek Cathedral in New York on 29 December 1946. He was forty-six, and she was seventeen.

Onassis soon had the heir he longed for. On 30 April 1948, in New York, his son was born. He was christened Alexander, after an uncle who had been killed by the Turks in Smyrna – and also after Alexander the Great. Shortly after the birth, Aristotle announced he was moving his base from America to Europe.

Onassis already had apartments and houses in Montevideo, Buenos Aires and New York. Now he acquired a villa on the outskirts of Athens, an apartment in the avenue Foch in Paris, and a gleaming white château with private beaches at the tip of Cap d'Antibes in the South of France. Shortly after, Tina gave birth to their second child, on 11 December 1950: a girl, whom they called Christina.

In the world of shipping, Stavros Niarchos was Onassis's arch rival. By 1949, the two Greeks were vying with each other to build the biggest fleet of oil tankers in the world. Between them, they precipitated a shipping boom of staggering proportions as the price of oil soared and tanker rates rose accordingly. Onassis complained that Niarchos hadn't got an original idea in his head and made his fortune by copying him. He was not amused when Niarchos married Tina's sister, Eugenie, bought a house near his own in New York and a château, like his, in the south of France. But what really angered him was Tina's admission that she thought Niarchos was in love with her.

In June 1953, Onassis had the great satisfaction of launching the biggest tanker in the world. His daughter, Christina, broke a bottle of champagne over the bows and his son, Alexander, pushed the button that sent it down the slipway. A year later, he pulled off another coup that surprised the world when he announced that he had acquired a 40 per cent interest in the Société des Bains de Mer at Monte Carlo, which controlled the principality's Casino, five hotels and other properties. Prince Rainier watched with mixed feelings as the Greek tycoon set up his headquarters overlooking Monte Carlo's lovely harbour.

Within a week of the Monte Carlo take-over, Onassis took delivery of the ship which was to become world renowned – the *Christina*. The 1700-ton yacht had been converted from a Canadian frigate and was now a showpiece of utter luxury. The bathrooms were of Sienna marble, with solid gold taps; there was a vast open fireplace inlaid with lapis lazuli, doors of antique Japanese lacquer, exquisite Russian icons and two El Greco paintings hanging behind Onassis's ornate desk. Eight speed boats and a five-seater amphibian aircraft were included; and the deck not only had a vast swimming pool, but a raised dance floor. The whole thing cost upwards of $1½ million a year to run.

Where did the children fit in? In his biography of Onassis, Peter Evans says neither Ari nor Tina took an active rôle as parents. Christina and Alexander lived in a world of pampered neglect, assigned to the care of nannies, secretaries and private tutors. Sometimes they did not see their parents for months. They were often left to eat alone, yet occasionally invited to lunch with some of the most famous people in the world – 'to gawk at Cary Grant or converse with Churchill'. Materially, they lived in a wonderland. As a result, Alexander would often throw spectacular tantrums and Christina, a plump, clumsy child retreated into a world of her own.

Onassis had been married for 11 years when he met Maria Callas. The tempestuous Greek prima donna had married Giovanni Battista Meneghini, a man old enough to be her father, who had masterminded her career and turned her from a myopic, overweight singer of small repute into a svelte, worldly woman of immense allure and stunning voice. Onassis did not reveal his interest in the diva until a year after their first meeting.

It was in 1957, when Callas made her debut at the Paris Opera. Throughout the day she received baskets of roses with messages of admiration, written in Greek but with no signature. Only the final delivery was signed, 'Aristotle Onassis'. In June 1959, he kept his promise to be in London for the opening of Callas's *Medea* and threw a supper party for her afterwards. Friends noticed that Aristotle's wife, Tina, was unusually subdued. The evening ended with a memorable photograph of Callas being embraced by both her husband, Meneghini, and Onassis.

Breaking point came when Callas and her husband accepted an invitation to join a cruise party on the *Christina*. Sir Winston and Lady Churchill were among the guests, as well as Fiat millionaire Umberto Agnelli and his wife. On the surface, the distinguished boatload enjoyed a wonderful three weeks in the Mediterranean; but there were hidden tensions. At one point, when the party had docked at Istanbul, Onassis and Callas disappeared for several hours. When they returned, Callas told her husband, 'I love Ari.'

Tina was not sure how serious the affair was until after the cruise. Then, when photographs of Onassis and Callas began to appear in all the papers, she feared the worst.

When Tina filed for divorce, her statement included a significant passage: 'It is almost 13 years since Mr Onassis and I were married in New York City. Since then he has become one of the world's richest men, but his great wealth has not brought me happiness with him, nor, as the world knows, has it brought him happiness with me.'

When Callas announced the end of her marriage Meneghini cursed both her and Onassis: 'I pity you, because you will both pay in hell for this.'

Those who expected Onassis to marry Callas were disappointed. He told close friends that he had a deep affinity with her, but had no intention of marrying her. (One obstacle was the fact that his children hated her – as they were later to hate Jackie Kennedy – and regarded her as responsible for the break up of their parents' marriage.) He seemed unsure of his feelings towards her and, at one point, even pleaded with Tina to reconsider divorce and go back to him. The prima donna was shattered when he told the Press, 'There was never any romance between Callas and myself.'

During the summer of 1960 Onassis was just as attentive to Callas as ever. They were seen dancing together and snuggling close over nightclub tables. But when Tina fractured a leg skiing in St Moritz, Ari rushed to her bedside with armfuls of flowers and renewed pleas for her to think again. But Tina had already embarked on another relationship and would soon marry a thirty-five-year-old English aristocrat, the Marquis of Blandford.

Maria Callas was no longer certain what she meant to Onassis, though she loved him desperately. She didn't want to sing any more, cancelled concerts at the last moment, and went for months without practicing a note. What she wanted more than anything was to be his wife, to have a home and some peace of mind; but Aristotle soon began to treat her with such unkindness that friends begged her to leave him before he broke her heart.

At this stage in his life Onassis believed that, materially, he had achieved everything he wanted. Now he had even had his own island, Skorpios, with a harbour for his yacht, a villa, a dozen luxurious guest chalets, stables and even a private telephone exchange. He began moving around with an ultra-chic crowd led by Princess Lee Radziwill, sister of Jackie Kennedy, the wife of US President John F. Kennedy.

Jackie Kennedy was suffering from deep depression after the death of her baby son, Patrick, born prematurely. When Aristotle heard this, he offered to put the *Christina* entirely at Jackie's disposal. Leaving Callas brooding in Paris, he stocked the yacht with caviar, the finest vintage wines and exotic fruits and took the First Lady on a cruise.

Onassis was in Hamburg launching a tanker when he learned of Kennedy's assassination in Dallas on 22 November 1963. He flew immediately to Washington, where he was welcomed as one of the few non-family mourners at the White House. After the funeral Jackie, a tragic, vulnerable figure, needed seclusion and privacy, and Onassis offered it to her aboard his yacht, on his private island or in the luxury of his homes around the world.

For the next few years, Jackie enjoyed his company and sympathy almost as though he were an elder statesman among her friends. There was great surprise, therefore, when, in October 1968, they announced they were to be married. Alexander and Christina Onassis were shattered by the news. Alexander remarked bitingly: 'It's a perfect match. My father loves names, and Jackie loves money.'

The wedding took place on the island of Skorpios. There was a fine drizzle which, according to the Greeks, meant good luck. Onassis's children sat sullenly together glaring at the bride, who looked girlish in her long sleeved ivory silk dress with a wide matching ribbon in her brown, shoulder length hair. The bridegroom, steel grey hair distinctive against his dark skin, could not mistake their feelings. The Kennedys, too, had been distinctively cool in their congratulations.

There was no doubt that the couple, themselves, went into the marriage with high hopes, and they appeared relaxed and in high spirits. Once the honeymoon was over, however, Onassis went back to the business deals that were his life's blood, and Jackie was left a great deal on her own. But business did not go so well for him after his marriage. There was some talk in international markets that Onassis was losing his touch; his old methods of wheeling and dealing not paying off in days of increasing high technology. In his private life, too, there were fleeting shadows of darker things to come.

On the evening of 3 May 1970, Eugenie Niarchos, his former wife's sister who had married his arch rival, took an overdose of seconol. Niarchos, himself, apparently tried desperately to revive her but failed, and before the doctor arrived she was dead. Scandal was in the air and Onassis made much of it, blaming Stavros Niarchos for Eugenie's death. It was his son, Alexander, who finally squared up to his father and told him to drop the whole bitter affair.

There were other tensions between father and son. Alexander was deeply in love with Baroness Fiona von Thyssen, one of the loveliest women in Europe. She was sixteen years older than the dark haired Onassis heir, who was slightly taller than his father and wore heavy, horn-rimmed spectacles. Their affair started when he was eighteen and she was thirty-three. Onassis made several subtle attempts to end the liaison, without success.

Onassis found that marrying a woman as famous as Jackie Kennedy had its drawbacks. Every move they made seemed to be public property. In his biography, *Jackie*, Willi Frischauer lays great emphasis on the shadow cast by John F. Kennedy. Former First Lady, Jackie, was still very much in demand by the media and for countless state functions, *not* as Mrs Onassis, but as the ex-Mrs Kennedy. As a fiercely proud Greek, Ari found that hard to live with.

Christina called her stepmother 'Madame', and to Alexander she was 'The Geisha'. It was not a happy situation. Jackie's answer to all her difficulties was to indulge her love of clothes. In the first year of her marriage she went on a compulsive shopping spree and spent $1¼ million in the fashion houses. She bought clothes by the carload, ordered dresses and jewels by the dozen; yet Onassis complained he never saw her in anything but a pair of jeans. Jackie's excesses didn't matter to him at first. He felt she had suffered greatly and needed to be indulged. But as she continued to plough through his money, Ari began to protest.

There were other signs that all was not well. Onassis discovered he had married a lady with a will of her own and who was not afraid to show it. Sometimes, he fled back to Maria Callas for comfort, but after one such visit, Jackie took an overdose of sleeping pills. She survived, but Ari realized things could never be the same between them again.

Looking to the future, Onassis was anxious for Christina to make the best possible marriage. As far as he was concerned, there could be no better choice than twenty-three-year-old Peter Goulandris, whose family were also in shipping. Christina liked Peter and, on five separate occasions, agreed to marry him – only to cancel the engagement party at the last minute. Without prior warning she married, instead, a forty-eight-year-old real estate man she had met in the swimming pool of the Hotel Metropole in New York. When Onassis received the news, he exploded. He made it clear that as long as Christina remained married, she would not receive a penny from the Onassis trust.

While he was still reeling from the news of Christina's marriage, Ari heard that his former wife, Tina, had secretly married Stavros Niarchos. Aristotle felt he had been betrayed. He went wild, and Jackie began to feel like an outsider. The difference between their two temperaments became insurmountable. Jackie, he complained, was 'cold hearted and shallow'. He felt cheated by his marriage and betrayed by his family. While she buried the deep hurt she felt, he let it be seen by the whole world. 'My God, what a fool I've made of myself,' he told friends.

On the evening of Sunday 21 January 1973, his son Alexander's Piaggio aircraft crashed on its take-off from Athens. Alexander was still alive when dragged from the wreckage, but all efforts to save him failed and he died the following day. Onassis's grief was so great that, at first, he would not part with Alexander's body for burial. But the worst part of his grief was guilt: Alexander had warned him that the Piaggio aircraft used by Onassis's airline, Olympic Airways, was a death trap.

Onassis tried to get over his overwhelming sense of loss by taking to the high seas with Jackie. She understood only too well what he was feeling. For a brief time, there was tenderness between them but, each night, Onassis walked the deck of the *Christina* alone. His insomnia became acute and he could not sleep at all in the dark. Back on Skorpios, he roamed the island until dawn and spent hours sitting besides his son's tomb.

Meanwhile, the marriage steadily deteriorated. Although Jackie felt pity for Onassis in his grief, they spent less and less of their time together and Jackie began to feel out of place in this intense Greek family. After a journey to Acapulco, where Jackie had spent her honeymoon with Jack Kennedy, she asked if he would buy her a house there. Choosing to feel insulted by this, he became difficult. It was in that mood that he wrote his will, leaving his fortune to Christina and almost cutting out his wife.

Since Alexander's death, Onassis had felt desperately tired. By the spring of 1974, he had difficulty keeping his eyes open or swallowing his food. When he consulted a specialist, he was told he had an illness called *myasthenia gravis*, a disease in which the body turns against itself, brought on by stress, fatigue and too much alcohol. It was incurable.

As the illness crept upon him he began to treat Christina as his successor, encouraging her interest in shipping. She showed surprising ability to grasp complexities, but her moods varied – once she had to be treated for an overdose of sleeping pills.

At the beginning of 1975 Onassis, still complaining about the way in which Jackie spent his money, asked for divorce proceedings to go ahead. Then, knowing the end was near, he flew to Paris, for treatment. The family – what was left of it – drew around him. He gave up the fight and died on 15 March. Christina was at his bedside, exhausted and under sedation. Jackie was at that moment detained in New York.

Christina had made a last gesture for her father's sake, an innocent deception that made him happy. She took Peter Goulandris to his bedside and told him they were going to be married. She had divorced Joseph Bolker, her first husband. There were to be three more marriages in her life. None of them worked. Nor could the Onassis millions save her from a tragically early death. By strange coincidence, she died in November 1988 in Argentina, where the young Greek from Smyrna had started it all.